J.P. Pelosi grew up in Sydney, Australia, in the 1980s and so was naturally obsessed with Han Solo, Reebok sneakers, Skittles and Pepsi ads. Nothing much has changed. He still lives in Sydney, now with his own family and works as a managing editor. His writing has covered travel, sports, film, finance, and business and has appeared in leading publications such as *The Guardian*, *The Atlantic*, *The Sunday Telegraph* and *The Sun Herald*. His short story *The Power of Parra's Fans* was also selected for ABC Book's *Unsung Sporting Heroes* collection.

Dedicated to my dad

J.P. Pelosi

CHOCOLATE CRACKLE SATURDAYS

AUSTIN MACAULEY PUBLISHERS™
LONDON • CAMBRIDGE • NEW YORK • SHARJAH

Copyright © J.P. Pelosi 2024

The right of J.P. Pelosi to be identified as author of this work has been asserted by the author in accordance with sections 77 and 78 of the Copyright, Designs and Patents Act 1988.

All rights reserved. No part of this publication may be reproduced, stored in a retrieval system, or transmitted in any form or by any means, electronic, mechanical, photocopying, recording, or otherwise, without the prior permission of the publishers.

Any person who commits any unauthorised act in relation to this publication may be liable to criminal prosecution and civil claims for damages.

All of the events in this memoir are true to the best of author's memory. The views expressed in this memoir are solely those of the author.

A CIP catalogue record for this title is available from the British Library.

ISBN 9781035838301 (Paperback)
ISBN 9781035838318 (ePub e-book)

www.austinmacauley.com

First Published 2024
Austin Macauley Publishers Ltd®
1 Canada Square
Canary Wharf
London
E14 5AA

Thanks to Mum for motivating me to take an interest in English literature and writing, and Dad for all of his lessons in soccer, food and old movies; my siblings for always making me laugh; my wife, Ash for her love and support; my son, Jake for his joy and humour; JC ('John') Abouchar for leading our many childhood adventures and his stellar comedic timing; Holy Family School for helping shape my early years and giving me a venue to fall in love with sport and Space Food Sticks; the Parramatta Eels for at least winning the comp when I was a kid, if not ever again since; and Pizza Hut for your wonderful restaurants that gave the 1980s a perfect lowly lit, garlic infused backdrop.

Introduction:
88 Miles Per Hour!

If I had my own time travelling DeLorean, I'd probably go back to the 1980s strangely enough, the period in which the car was created. I'd punch in 26 October 1985, the exact same date Marty McFly returns from his trip to the fifties in the iconic film, *Back to the Future*. That point in time seems about the peak of pop culture for me. The reason for this is obvious—I was nine years old in '85! At that age, everything seems possible. All the entertainment and culture around you feels infinitely big. Trends stick like popped bubble gum on your face. You lose perspective because you have none in the first place. This is so much so that you regard whipping your fringe up into an impossible mass of gel as a rite of passage, not just something that bothers your mother. In '85, I'd have typically laid back on my *Empire Strikes Back* doona and flicked through my favourite Bullwinkle and Rocky comic book hoping that at least one more Cadbury Furry Friends was in the pantry. I loved those colourful cartoon animal wrappers, especially when you might score one of your favourites such as Barry Buffalo or Donny Dingo.

On other days, my siblings and I would come inside from tearing around the yard of our Lindfield home, a quiet and leafy suburb on Sydney's north shore, to be greeted by mum with a plate of Iced Vovos. On a cloudless day after a long spin on our skateboards and scooters, she might have offered a pine-orange Paul's Popper or an apple Just Juice. The Cottees company also made what we considered to be a sublime caramel syrup for ice cream, which we actually poured into our milkshakes, and stirred up with a Breville mixer. Sometimes we even added a bit of the chocolate flavour too, imagining we were the first kids ever in suburbia to do so. Later on, we'd see friends mix Fanta and Sprite, suggesting child-aged mixologists were in fact everywhere at the time. We shared pop culture with our peers seemingly by telepathy.

Our home was open and spacious for the time, built in the fifties with wonderful hardwood floors that my dad polished many times himself, usually on his hands and knees with a tin of lacquer and a brush, a small Sony transistor radio playing a Roy Orbison or Mario Lanza song in the background. There was a lot of light in the house, particularly, in the front room which you could enter from three sides through clear glass doors, perhaps to sit and listen to a large Panasonic hi-fi system or flick through an array of colourful coffee table books. It was the sort of home we would sprint around in our footy socks, getting from one end of the house where the bedrooms were, up through the hallway, past the front door, the well-lit front room and up to the kitchen to grab some lime cordial.

On a hot day, our leafy garden filled with wattle and wisteria flowers, kumquats, lemon and liquid amber trees, and the smell of rosemary and lavender, was a wonderful haven to play and keep cool. Though Sydney's summers could be pretty harsh and we often needed a little more help to chill out—ice, ideally. Luckily, our local shops were a five-minute walk up the road, so we could stroll up together with mum or dad and secure a few Cool Shark ice blocks made by Streets for 45 cents each. The pointed blue ice on a stick, ironically shaped like a man-eating shark, was a delicious blend of flavours that the advertisers claimed was 'a real cool bite of lemonade and creaming soda.' What brilliant ideas the adults at the time had, I thought.

For me, those mid-eighties represent a whir and a blur of pink neon, pop music perfection, vibrant video game pixels, whizzing sports cars, slick hair and large sunglasses. It was all about bright colours, big sounds, high tech and grand ideas. It was pretty great. Now I'm certainly aware that the height of pop culture for each of us depends on our age and the time in which we grew up. And for some, the ongoing changes in culture might actually be more interesting than what they experienced as a kid. I know many people like this—they refuse to look back, preferring to go with the belief that everything new is better. That point of view is fine and, in fact, is possibly less problematic than those of us who long for the past and all its retro glory.

Still, I can't get beyond the idea that my childhood was marked by bold and often radical concepts, many of which transformed our lives. Some were silly, others were daring, and many were apparently, the result of some very loosely run brainstorms and too many Mentos chased by Coca-Cola. But things were tried folks, that is the point. Boundaries were pushed and in many instances, the propositions that saw the light of day were kind of wacky—like that creepy talking bear who looked like he was on acid, Teddy Ruxspin. Teddy might have been a bestseller but his beady eyes gave my Pound Puppy the heebie-jeebies! Or how about the Teenage Mutant Ninja Turtles? Me and my brother Andy loved those bizarre-looking ninja-skilled weirdos, though I recognise to our parents such odd toys might have indicated the need for a federal enquiry. In some ways, it was really the start of modern times, at least as we now know them, what with talking bears, turtles that eat pizza and time travelling sports cars. Who could deny such innovation? All this is what I retrospectively love about growing up and it's why I'd take my plutonium-filled DeLorean back to the eighties, to a time marked by wild hair, furry headbands, blindingly white sneakers, larger-than-necessary logos, thigh-hugging short shorts, pillow-thick pizzas, jumbo-sized soft drinks, ostentatious sports cars that were oddly always raspberry red, digital gadgets with too many buttons, skateboarding without helmets, BMX riding (without helmets!), bright, buzzing and addictive board games, loud and lewd action movies relentlessly billed as 'blockbusters,' electronically enhanced music, double denim, double mint gum, Double Dragon and toys that seem like they were concocted by teenagers revved up on too much Mello Yello. Take us back dear DeLorean, to rejoin the family outing in dad's bulky old Volvo station wagon, en route to a darkened fast-food joint with cosy faux leather booths, a night of pan-fried Pizza Hut pizza and endless soft drink top-ups, beneath a cool autumn night and a brightly flickering sign that read, *open.*

I suppose this is a very American ideal that came with the 'sell' of suburban utopia. While that's a notion spawned well before the eighties, such ideals and Americana were everywhere during our childhood. Despite 12,000 kilometres of ocean separating us, Sydney's suburbia never seemed too far away from Hollywood, really. I mean we had all the mega-budget mega-movies in our mega-cinemas, the best blinking, and beeping toys in our shops and the most sugar-heavy American cereals in our super-duper-markets. There was never any doubt as to which nation's cultural footprint was the world's most impactful, as all of its invention and accompanying philosophy was thrust upon us willing consumers in the 1980s. Just as it was with the theme from *Charles in Charge,* we couldn't get enough of it. To achieve this, America's powerbrokers let creators run wild and this freedom led to some iconic brands, beloved stories, and timeless iconography. How else do you think they came up with *Alf,* a cat-eating alien who settles in comfortably with a suburban family? Or how about Michael Jackson's *Thriller* video? Something tells me that wouldn't have worked a decade earlier. This stuff, combined with a few local gems and of course many British favourites, filled our lives with a touch of flair and frivolity. This is what I want to recall here, with a cultural sensibility but also as a tribute.

Finally, this feels a very timely exercise because the kids of today appreciate the eighties too. For example, they're widely adopting its music, sporting its sneakers and peering over its Ray Ban sunglasses. They know the classic films of the era and many of them are getting about on eighties-style skateboards. Yes, like it or not, the eighties have arrived… again. Why not? It was a simpler time and yet everything around us was just a bit slicker. There was hyper-colour and flashing lights on the machines within our homes. There were brave movements atop fluorescent-coloured plastic wheels and at the helm of a Nintendo Entertainment System. Photos were instant and TV was static-covered and neon bright. It was a time of big swings, where even the whiffs connected. It was modern but still retained some of the traditions of the past. Listen, the eighties weren't perfect. But they left an impression that's still resonating decades later and that's got to mean something.

So, rev up that DeLorean gang, we're heading back to a red-letter day—a pop culture peak, if you will. After all, if you're going to travel back in time, why not do it with some style, to paraphrase the great Doc Brown.

At Home in the Eighties

When I was about ten, I worked out how to climb up on the roof of our family home. There was a perfectly placed mulberry tree right outside our kitchen window, which I likely noticed one day while devouring some lunchtime sausage rolls. I just had to explore whatever leverage it might offer, I decided. Soon, I was halfway up the tree, having launched onto from a nearby side gate, and despite the purple stain of mulberry juice on some toes, finally got high enough that I could haul myself up over the drain onto the roof tiles. There I sat, proud as purple punch, surveying the garden before me, our dog looking up with a bewildered face, wondering how one of her previously earthbound friends had learned to fly.

While up there I prowled the surface for lost balls and frisbees, typically propelled too high for anyone to legitimately attempt a catch and landing too far away to be easily retrieved. This was a problem the neighbourhood over apparently, because standing on those red tiles, I could see a number of shabby old tennis balls and flying discs lodged in the cracks, beneath twigs and leaves or tentatively off the edge of Lindfield's varied residential roofing. While I couldn't get to those roofs, I made it my duty to scoop up as many of the lost items atop our house, perhaps hoping to rekindle so many interrupted games—tennis with a net made out of metal garden chairs, California Games-style frisbee distance toss, touch football using a miniature league ball, cricket with a golf ball, baseball with a super bouncy ball, Aussie rules with an imitation red rubber ball from the service station, basketball three-point contests, World Cup soccer shootouts, Nerf-weapon shootouts, water balloon fights, and of course, paper aeroplane contests. All of this is to say that we really did make the best of our play time growing up, sometimes to the detriment of preserving our thirty-something house.

It was a solid little castle though, one well built for four eighties-era kids with an appetite for testing the top speed of a go-kart, who were deadeyes with a water pistol, and unfazed by the sight of a heavy marble punching a hole in one of mum's windows. Though we were alarmed by the sound of dad rumbling down the hall like Homer Simpson should we have connected with his car. Both the wildly misplaced bravado and brief moments of guilt during childhood are rarely forgotten, mostly because the balance is so inverted during adulthood. We long for the clear-minded joy that once allowed us to scale jagged mulberry trees up onto slanted roofs.

I also remember sitting in my family living room sporting all-white leather Reebok sneakers and a pair of brightly patterned surfing shorts, watching dad perform a magic show for my birthday party in front of my similarly dressed little friends. We all relaxed on the rug or on the avocado green sofa chomping on Milky Ways and Crunchie bars while dad moved about the stage—the floor in front of our old boxy NEC TV and bulky VCR player below—in a fake magician's hat and moustache, no less. There were rows of black video tapes nearby, a couple of which were actually purchased from a shop, not taped directly from the television like most of them. One of which was an early version of the first *Star Wars* film released in 1977, though if my memory serves me correctly, we didn't have it until the eighties. As such, everything *Star Wars* related occurred for us in the 1980s. That's just how things worked.

There were also board games nearby, like Monopoly, Trivial Pursuit and Pictionary, but don't forget the Rubik's Cube or our stack of records and tapes in the living room stereo cabinet. Just outside the door, the front yard was strewn with a couple of recently ridden bicycles and little plastic toy cars to pedal around in, plus my well-worn Reflex skateboard, the sort of vehicle every cool cat was getting around on, typically decorated with an array of stickers featuring skulls, snakes, spiders, or zombies. I mean the mid-eighties were particularly radical. In fact, you might recall that everything was 'totally rad.' Those BMX bikes with their chunky tyres and small rubber handles were rad. So too were stereos with oversized speakers and big buttons. Even the microwave ovens with their black glass doors were so bloody rad. I don't want to overstate it, but there was some real style even if at times there wasn't much substance. Come on, wasn't *Magnum PI* premium content? How about *Cheers? Family Ties? The Facts of Life?* Netflix executives are surely salivating as they read off these hit titles. We watched them all, breaking up the comedy with action from the likes of *MacGyver*, *21 Jump Street* and *Voltron*.

We'd colour the Incredible Hulk with Crayola crayons, watch Prince, Billy Joel and Madonna perform on *Video Hits* and wait for mum to bring us hot pizza subs from the microwave, the frozen variety topped full of cabanossi slices, pineapple and something akin to beef but perhaps closer to shredded tyre. Who cared, we had a two-litre Sunkist in the fridge ready to pour into our plastic *Return of the Jedi* cups. We each have our own versions of this recollection, but I know that for those of us in eighties living rooms, the memories are similarly buoyed by the whimsy of great toys and trinkets, cheesy TV shows and dreams of being as cool as Andrew McCarthy.

In retrospect, all this new entertainment led to a feeling that our lives were abuzz with possibility. We were big-haired jitterbugs dancing to a new beat and hanging on like—and with—our Russell Fanta and Sprite yo-yos. These were head-spinning times, folks.

The BMX bike was perhaps the most transformative of items. Yes, the sorts of speedy jumps, off-road trickery, and wheelie action synonymous with BMX riding actually began years before we zipped into a frame, and some cursory internet research confirms that sales of the Schwinn Stingray accelerated in the seventies. Its long handles and raised seat were apparently piloted by little rascals all around sunny California first, such freewheeling fun an early foray into two-wheeled wizardry that we came to know with BMXs. But let's be honest, cooler kids hitting handmade dirt ramps and skidding through the mud usually occurred behind the more slick-looking handlebars of the BMX. Indeed, the style and showmanship of BMX riding were synonymous with the boisterous sporting tastes of the time. And so was the BMX banditry, as it was shaped by little retro-era riders everywhere, pavement pirates with a preference for trucker hats and yellow t-shirts as well as a biking bravado not previously seen. Load up the 1983 hit film *BMX Bandits* with a very young Nicole Kidman, if you don't believe me. Listen, we also know that the International BMX Federation started in 1981, and the first championships were held in '82, so presumably, it all wasn't too official before then, anyway. Whatever your view of the history, it's certainly true that in Sydney at least, real BMX brats didn't screech onto the streets until the early eighties, and boy did we love it.

Most holiday stretches were filled with long hot days gripping those soft rubber handles until they reached melting point, as we flew through fence-lined neighbourhoods perched just inches above the tapered saddles of our two-wheeled beasts. Oh the wheels, whooshing beneath the bright blue, red and green painted frames reflecting in the sun, as we explored the varied alleys of suburbia and the limits of our spirit.

One day in December of 1986, we set off on one of our many high-spirited missions. The summer sun lingered, causing our shirts to stick. But the wind cooled our heads as we careened down our neighbour's driveway. Our adventures were dictated by how far we might be compelled to pedal, be it the corner shop, the school grounds, the local footy field or further out to the shopping mall. We'd often venture to the private golf course, me, Andy, and our neighbourhood mate John, who loved to hatch plans for holiday capers. Our regular racket over at the golf club was no exception. For a trio of hopeful BMX bandits, each fuelled by Allen's Strawberry Creams and Polly Waffles, the pristine grounds of the seemingly upper-class golf club were like a porch light to wayward flies. The ride over was easy, cutting through a few narrow laneways that split several of the avenues in our quiet corner of Lindfield. We'd eventually reach a more open stretch and a series of downhill runs until we hit the long bend of Earl Street, just past the bus stop. There, beyond a small grass embankment, some ambitious soul had cut a hole at the base of the wire fence surrounding the grounds (was any wire fence spared in the eighties?) Past the chain-links lay thick bushland that resembled a jungle, flickering with the sort of wild possibility we'd witnessed in the movie *Predator*. Of course, while an alien with superhuman strength and a creepy laugh was fun on celluloid, I really didn't want to see him in real life! Not without Arnie by our sides and the promise of a rescue chopper.

John stepped forward. He was a bit of a maverick, a smart-arse who either earned a quick verbal victory or got us in deep crap fast. Luckily, his quick wit was usually enough to disarm those who confronted us, like a rival group of bike riders on the other side of our suburb. We once squared off outside the local retirement home when John shut down their ringleader by asking if he'd purchased his rather colourful shirt from a well-known women's clothing shop, Susan's. Any eleven-year-old will tell you that from this there's rarely a fitting comeback. The Colourful Shirt Gang was nowhere in sight on this day, thankfully. We could focus on the task at hand. I checked my backpack. Supplies were as integral to the mission as the action itself: strawberry bubble-gum check. Torch—check. Plastic water pistol—check. Duct tape from Dad's tool box—check. Walkman—check. If you were really industrious, you might have drawn up a map and set of plans, blue pencil for locations, and red for the roads.

John and Andy dropped to their haunches like little ninjas, so as not to be seen. We'd been told off by several grumpy plaid-panted golfers—possibly distraught with their taste in clothing—so quickly learned that it was best to stay off the manicured lawns. We darted under the fence and slid down a short stony incline to the creek, splashing into the shallow water, dirtying up our canvas Converse sneakers like an army platoon into a dirty jungle river. In suburbia this was the best footwear for any suburban jungle drop because they were light and tough, but mostly because they made us look like the kids from the movie *Stand by Me*. A pink ball glistened in the water, so I skipped over a few stones and scooped it up, then tossed it to John. A small bag full of balls might secure us $5, which could go towards any number of things, including a six-pack of Coke, a Van Damme movie from the video store, even a Nintendo game we'd been saving for like Metal Gear. Failing that, we'd go cart to cart and sell them back to the self-proclaimed golfing legends in goofy pants.

Missions like this were made possible by our two-wheeled time machines which zapped us forward to the boundaries of our immediate world, allowed us to escape like souped-up getaway cars and, most importantly, delivered us home just in time for lamb chops on the dinner table.

Fast Cars for Fast Times

The lure of moving at speed was also the stuff of our daydreams. In the school playground at Holy Family Primary in Lindfield, fantasies of driving fast cars were only topped by the possibility of scoring a pack of Hubba Bubba or a bag of chocolate milk buds. Our little school was a short bus ride away from home, set on a straight stretch at the northern end of the Pacific Highway, so the chance to see a few choice vehicles careening by was pretty high. We typically waited by the fence with bated breath. What was it about great cars back then? I've heard pundits like Joe Rogan say the eighties-era cars were awful, but he's a revhead and possibly talking about performance. I don't care about that Joe! I'm here for shallow eighties-era aesthetics, that's what it's all about when you're an eight-year-old. Think Tubbs and Crocket in that white Ferrari Testarossa of *Miami Vice*, the silver Porsche 928 in which Tom Cruise tore around Chicago in *Risky Business*, or the black Pontiac Trans Am that was fitted out for KITT in *Knight Rider*. All of these were beautiful-looking cars—I don't need to know their ability to handle in the wet or their maximum speeds on a straight stretch. I just know as every kid did at the time, that these vehicles looked otherworldly and evoked the possibility that they could transport their pilots into other dimensions.

Robert Zemeckis's time-travelling DeLorean did just that, and to this day when I'm lucky enough to spot one of those futuristic cars, my imagination runs wild. And I say this knowing full well that the car's creator, John DeLorean, did not put his best work into that particular vehicle. So what? All you'd need to remedy the relatively low performance of a DeLorean, if you have one in the garage that is, is to give your old science teacher a holler and ask him to hook you up with some quantum tubing to circulate your magnetic flux…oh, and some plutonium.

Problem solved, your DeLorean should now propel you into other time periods upon hitting the requisite miles per hour. But that space age DeLorean wasn't the only car I pined for as a kid. As most mums and dads will recall, the car that stood out above all others in the mid-eighties was the Lamborghini Countach. This Italian masterpiece might have actually been built to travel through time *without* plutonium— how else can you explain the inclusion of its racing-style spoiler? Who devised this thing anyway, the X-Men? It's a downright marvel of engineering and design that can only be rivalled by the Fender electric guitar or the Air Jordan 5 basketball sneaker. Go pop on the eighties film *Cannonball Run* and watch the opening four minutes. The black Countach racing along the open highway, revving and whirring away from the pursuing cops is an absolute thrill for the senses. It literally looks like it's about to launch into the Californian sky. Had they left the driver to her own devices it just might have. The cops in the movie are said to be in pursuit of the car for two hours because, well, they have zero chance of catching it. This '85 version was the third iteration of the Countach and the man behind its design was Marcello Gandini. It had 455 horsepower and a 5.2 litre, 12-cylinder V-12 engine. To put that into perspective for the non-motor heads, your average car in the suburban driveway has about 180 horsepower and about a 1.8-2 litre engine. But ultimately this was about the look, at least for us kids. When we saw a Countach cruise down the highway, and I think it happened just once, the aircraft-like nature of its metal body and the tubular frame looked completely unreal. The thing was, the car was wide but very low to the ground, meaning as it came towards you, it seemed to be a hovering spacecraft. And the doors scissored up like a UFO's cockpit too, so if you were lucky enough to ever see a driver emerge, chances were he or she was a robot or maybe an alien. Would that alien creature be hostile or come armed with a weird slimy contagion?

Maybe, the word Countach apparently means just that. But its true use, in Piedmontese slang, is to express amazement.

The bold, over the top, audacious design of the Countach was indeed amazing and surely was made this way to cut through the atmosphere at nearly 300 kilometres per hour. The prices on these cars vary, but as far as I can tell $100,000 in the mid-eighties would have secured one, which seems outrageous when an Audi Spyder today costs about four times that. Listen, we can work in inflation but on the eight-year-old's eye test, I know which car I'd rather—the one that just returned from a Mars mission.

The last vehicle I'd like to mention here is Condorman's Condormobile. Didn't see that coming, did you? Thought I was going with Batmobile? Look, the Batmobile is great and it's parked in a dark spooky cave every evening, so who am I to question its place in the pantheon of cool cars? Only that it's a vehicle that has existed through many decades and in different forms, whereas the Condormobile—an elaborately decorated Volkswagen Sterling Nova—was unique to the eighties, blasting across cinema screens in 1981. *Condorman* might have been a low-budget B-grade endeavour with a small following, but when that car outran a bunch of creepy spies in black Porsches, it was about the coolest thing my five-year-old mind could comprehend. Did cars like this actually exist? I wondered. More to the point, how is it that eighties superheroes were all such skilled drivers?

A Tech-Tonic Shift

The technology we had as kids was fairly pedestrian by today's standards and yet nothing like the proliferation of gadgets and appliances that sprung up in the eighties had ever occurred before. There were TVs in all shapes and sizes, futuristic video game consoles such as the Commodore and the Sega Master System, walkie-talkies, the Apple Mac home computer, Casio digital watches, Polaroid cameras, VCRs, boom boxes, cordless phones, handheld video cameras, talking toys and handheld gaming devices like the Gameboy were among some of the great tech items that hit the market at the time. And yet perhaps none were as remarkable as that little music in a box—the Sony Walkman.

The Walkman is said to have made its official appearance on shop shelves in 1979 after one of Sony's head honchos sought a portable way to listen to opera music other than the standard cassette tape recorder. But it took a little while for sales to climb and when they did, it was on like Donkey Kong! A little peek into the Walkman revolution as written widely online tells us that 50,000 units were sold in Japan in the first two months, when Sony had anticipated selling just 5,000! Soon enough many thousands were being sold and this quickly turned into millions.

Kids and teenagers especially gravitated towards the personalisation that the Walkman afforded them, seeing them hop onto a bus or on a skateboard, earphones on, music blasting and the rest of the world a mere backdrop. It was sort of a statement and certainly, a way to let others know that you weren't in the mood for chat, you had tunes to get through. This wasn't an outcome that some liked, of course, and critics soon questioned the necessity for isolating oneself, fearing that everyday conversation could die a quick death. Sounds familiar, doesn't it? Google some old pics of people wearing Walkman in the eighties and what's evident is that there were many of us sitting right next to each other but not paying attention to anything around us. The all-consuming nature of personal tech really took off at this point in time, many years before anyone had even heard of a smartphone.

The other factor here was accessibility—the Walkman was expensive in 1980 at about $150 in the US. But that really doesn't sound like much given the way today's tech is priced. For people earning a decent enough amount of money, the Walkman was within reach and this helps to explain why more than 400 million of the things have now sold all up. In my house, we loved any portable tape player though it would be a while before we scored the Sony version. A number of copycats followed as you can imagine and this made the product more accessible at least. There were loads of them, from the likes of Sanyo, Aiwa and Toshiba, to TEAC, JVC and Panasonic. There were silver ones, black ones, blue ones and even maroon. It all felt like the real thing when we were eight or nine, so I didn't sense anything different as The Bangles,' 'Walk like an Egyptian' got a workout on my silver and black 'Auto Reverse' Sanyo cassette player with bright orange earphones. Eventually, we convinced Mum and Dad that we needed a WM-F77 Sony model in our home—that was the black one, very slick with silver buttons and an AM/FM display on the front window. There was just something special about the Walkman that holds a place in our hearts, even beyond chowing down on microwave oven-cooked frozen pizza, scolding your Gameboy because Tetris was too hard, or making a calculation on your new Casio calculator watch while leaping into the family station wagon, hoping it might actually rocket along the road faster than Jake and Elwood's Blues mobile. The Walkman came with street cred and it never left it, even as it morphed into other versions of itself.

Despite 83 million selling in 1989 (as per Forbes.com), cassette tapes obviously didn't endure. Replaced promptly by the compact disc in 1990, tapes were very much of their time. However, their limitations didn't quash their ability to transcend everyday practicality — the 'mix tape' was a cultural staple of the eighties and a motif that still pleases people today. The reason being, it was the first time the home music listener could become a DJ, choosing the songs they wanted and in their own order so that the end result was a masterpiece in curation. That was the intention anyway and like a bouquet or a box of chocolates, the mix tape transitioned into the romantic settings to a rousing reception. Suitors of all ages would organise music for the eye of their affection with a perfectly concocted tape, a mix of the songs they felt best encompassed their would-be relationship, or simply the fact that they were very much looking forward to the prospect of sitting in the back row of the movie theatre with said person.

For younger mixers, the goal was simply to come up with a compilation that could beat your last one. And there was a range of ways to go about putting one together. For me the best approach was to sit by the radio during the Sunday afternoon Top 40 and wait for my favourite tracks, then scramble to hit both the play and record buttons to get in as much of the song as possible. The trick with this was to wait for a second or two as each song led in because hosts such as Shadoe Steven and Rick Dees liked to give a little intro spiel, eating into your taping. And so I'd wait, a beat…one, two… two-buttons-down! Some of the more memorable tracks I put down included a sweet collection in '87 that featured Michael Jackson's 'I Just Can't Stop Loving You,' George Michael's 'Faith,' Los Lobos' 'La Bamba,' George Harrison's 'Got My Mind Set On You,' Whitney Houston's 'I Wanna Dance With Somebody' and topping out with Starship's 'Nothing's Gonna Stop Us Now.' You couldn't make a bad mix tape with songs like that, not unless you slipped up in an overly panicked button thrust, or worse still, you ambitiously tried recording halfway into a tape, forgetting it was a 60-minute TDK and not the more luxurious 90-minute variety. This hiccup wasn't the end of the world, but you certainly had to think fast. Was it worth flipping and continuing on side B? Or was the opening track on the other side too special to give up? Tough one, but hey, 'When The Going Gets Tough, The Tough Get Going,' as the great Billy Ocean claimed in 1986, on his way to No. 1 in both Australia and the UK. Certainly, a mix-worthy song if ever there was one.

Taking Part

Birthday parties were filled with both dread and joy because who knew what hoops your pal's parents might have you leap through in nineteen-eighty-something. On the one hand, it might have been pin the tail on the donkey and pass the parcel, which was sufficient. A lesser event might have had you bobbing for apples and ducking a limbo stick. On the other hand, you might have been off to the video game arcade, ice rink or even an amusement park—special treats.

Excursions beyond the home always intrigued us and I'm pleased to see these sorts of parties have become popular again today. For example, many eighties families also turned to the relatively comfortable bowling alley, given it put a rowdy and rambling group of kids in one place that could absorb their chaos. Others liked the outdoors of putt, where presumably the weekend warrior mums and dads could also slice a few fluorescent balls over-elaborate water hazards. And a smaller group still went to the local ice rink for some out-of-control speed skating to Bon Jovi and Motley Crue ballads—a strange combination of movement and sound as there ever was. This also still happens, but in warmer climates like ours rinks are a little hard to come by…as are eighties rock songs that haven't yet been driven into the ground by modern TV advertisers.

But perhaps no eighties birthday celebration was better than a simple park gathering to play touch football, followed by a routine scarfing down of frankfurts and chocolate crackles. Touch footy was a proper sport, allowing the ultra-competitive seven-year-olds like myself to practice the moves I made up in the front yard. I did Steve Mortimer's chip and chase, but typically sent the ball further to fool eager beaver tippers. Or I tried Benny Elias's dummy and spin, though was one dummy really enough? I also liked to catch a deep kick on the full and then scramble past diving defenders like Slippery Steve Morris. If you could pull that one off your status as a footy legend on such Chocolate Crackle Saturdays was forever sealed. One afternoon at the park for Matt Flynn's party, a school mate, I wowed the rugby-loving parents in attendance with a fearless punt reception, forward charge, chip and chase combo.

I still recall Matt's dad sidling up to me after the match by the jelly-filled orange halves. He had some encouraging words but also wanted to lure me from soccer to rugby. He thought I'd make a good half-back, apparently. I thanked him and said I'd think about it, knowing full well that a kid my size might have better luck in a karate dojo (at least if you take a blow you land on a mat, right?) Conveniently touch footy was also a game of short sprints and sidesteps, which meant the sporty among us could excel even with limited football experience. The glory of victory at a footy-focused party also carried over into the schoolyard come Monday, where those kids who attended the last shindig would regale the best moves of the day…and perhaps the most legendary chocolates or lollies afterwards.

Birthday parties could also centre around movies and in my little mind, the sports party was only rivalled by the sports movie party. This simply included the screening of a flick that any sports-obsessed kid could get behind, classics such as *Hoosiers, Major League, Mighty Ducks* and the grossly underappreciated Goldie Hawn vehicle, *Wildcats*. I was also up for any film that included a sporting contest within it, even if the core storyline was something closer to teenage summer love, high school hijinx or goofy adventures in a haunted forest. One such movie was the legendary eighties action power piece, *Top Gun*, in which Tom Cruise and Val Kilmer took to the beach volleyball court for a heated contest between rival colleagues. Why would any film producer want to include this type of scene in a movie about fighter pilots? Well, I can only assume that like us sports nuts at home, these filmmakers also love a sporting battle squeezed into any scenario. That the scene is just minutes long is inconsequential—it stayed with us a long time, turning any outdoor moment into a chance for shirtless volleyball and high-fives. I mean my buddies and I surely didn't hand out high-fives with as much purpose until *Top Gun* came around.

There were also movies that had very little to do with sports but somehow still worked a sporting motif into proceedings and here John Cusack's *One Crazy Summer* comes to mind. In it, a down-and-out teenager Hoops McCann goes away for his summer holidays with a few pals and as you'd expect, ends up confronting the pretty boy bad guy. But there's no dust up here, just a basketball shootout. Of course, our hero can't really play basketball—in spite of his name— and subsequently throws up a few clankers to lose the respect of well, almost everyone in the movie. Similarly searching for respect on the basketball court is Scott Howard, aka *Teen Wolf*. Michael J. Fox's iconic eighties turn as a wolf boy point guard is a wonderful tale of what one can achieve when transformed into a teenage werewolf. I used to love the fact that Fox's character gives up on his wolfness near the end and convinces his basketball team mates that they can succeed without his fandangled superpowers. I mean it's really a coming-of-age story about a boy and a girl, a boy and his dad, and a boy dealing with too much facial hair. But the film's gripping sports subplot is what hooked me and many other kids at the time, I'm sure.

Even as I got older and turned to thrillers, action adventures and courtroom dramas, I still found myself gravitating towards those that mentioned sport. Think about it: these characters boasted rapid-fire one-liners and cool wardrobes but also loved to catch the occasional ball game. There's basic accessibility to that characteristic, I think. For instance, Matthew Broderick's Ferris Bueller loves baseball and the Chicago Cubs; Ralph Macchio's *Karate Kid* sports a San Diego Chargers jersey; *and* Chevy Chase's *Fletch* is a Lakers fanatic. There are many more but I think you get the point. When you're a kid, you look for cues and it's funny how often our favourite movies provide them.

Salami and Soccer

It took a while, but soccer or *football*, as the good people on SBS call it—has become pretty popular in Sydney. I mean few sports clubs the world over could boast as spirited a fan base as that of the Western Sydney Wanderers. Their closest rivals and regular A-League champs, Sydney FC, have also roused a strong following. This is pleasing, of course, but somewhat surprising. As kids of a Neapolitan father, we grew up to love soccer and yet neither our peers nor the community at large felt the same way. We lived in a city that in the early eighties not only lacked proper Neapolitan-style pizza but, you know, genuine multiculturalism. As such, being Italian back then was hardly as exotic as it is today, even with the likes of Madonna and Ralph Macchio waving the Red, White and Green for all of us. Sydney, like many places at the time, was sadly stuck in its ways. This meant that amaretti cookies were inferior to Tim Tams and soccer (or 'wogball') was the much poorer cousin of rugby.

It's strange to recall this now, as I listen to people in hipster inner city bars tell me where to buy the best cannoli or those in Circular Quay pubs advise which *football* team has the most talented midfield. It boggles the mind to think you can exist in the same space and time when a salami sandwich is condemned with Gordon Ramsey-like rage but then regarded as a culinary delight. When the shape of a ball can impact your social standing at primary school but eventually become the toy of choice at Bondi Beach. Hey, what can I tell you? In a world of short attention spans, it turns out we also have very short memories! This is human nature, of course, and has been for centuries, ever since the British docked tall ships into foreign ports with the same ease John Mayer's number is punched into the iPhones of available starlets. New York underwent a similar transition in the early twentieth century, during which time newcomers like the Jews and Italians were viewed with contempt because of their looks, behaviour and tastes. And yet, their combined impact on the cultural fabric of the world's greatest city would finish second to none. It's almost impossible to walk the streets of New York without noting a link to one or the other's heritage. But this type of marination takes time and is no better illustrated than in the sporting world.

So, during the eighties, my brother Andy and I forged a bond with soccer because Dad had nurtured us with it. And yet, our passion was in vain, in a part of the world where other games were not only dominant but a virtual religion. Meanwhile, those associated with soccer, like those who enjoyed small goods, were subject to a spicy form of ridicule. In the current era of expensive academies and rep squads and endless devotion to international mega-clubs like Barcelona and Manchester City, this perhaps seems impossible. I get it. But I assure you that soccer stars, let alone Italian soccer stars, were pretty much pariahs when we were kids.

Thankfully, Italian soccer is now rather admired Down Under. I'm not saying Aussies barrack for Italy in any way, in fact, things get pretty heated when the two nations play. But there's at least an appreciation for the skills of Italy's best. So, it's in this boggy midfield that my emotions become mixed about eighties soccer because, on the one hand, I loved growing up at a time when my own football skills were rather unique and I also felt ideally placed to appreciate the likes of Italian winger Bruno Conti when my peers couldn't (or wouldn't). This perspective is certainly limited to kids of immigrants growing up in places that don't see things the same way—and that can be a powerful memory.

It's possibly nice to reflect on this now because things have changed so much. Consider that an Italian player in the current era, such as Alessandro Del Piero, could be so coveted by fans in a city like Sydney, as evidenced by his signing to play for Sydney FC for a whopping $2 million back in 2012. This surely paved the way for others from the homeland to be remunerated for their footballing prowess with more than fresh bags of tortellini. Former Italian international Alessandro Diamanti signing on with Western United in 2019 comes to mind. Yes, Sydney has indeed shifted and there's a bit of validation for us, I won't lie. All those soccer balls booted around the front yard and up onto the roof were not a waste of time, after all. They played a small role in building new relationships and expanding our local culture. Like New York's great minestrone-matzo melting pot, we might have finally come together.

With all that said, I wouldn't trade my formative years on the soccer field for anything. The style of game we were taught by Dad stood out like Kevin Keegan's outrageous mop top. We didn't just hit the field eager to chase the ball around like hunting foxes, as eight and nine-year-old kids are wont to do, but rather read the play, stopped the ball, pushed it down the wing and pinpointed crosses. From an early age, we were able to showcase some skills most other kids in our comp hadn't been taught. The emphasis was on ball control, finding space and passing, ideas that are widely shared at junior camps everywhere now, but in the under nines in 1984 were about as prevalent as half-time apples. Like the oranges shared at the break, our Holy Family jerseys were oddly bright, though neatly trimmed with two green stripes down one side and a green collar.

Come to think of it, maybe someone wanted us to look like little oranges newly plucked from a tree. If not intimidating it surely must have been distracting. Apparently, our uniform designer was a bit on the fringe and so was our play. It didn't matter, with Dad's dedication to tactical football, there was no stopping our little squad—we cleaned up rival clubs like Berowra, Hornsby Heights and Bannockburn like Arsenal tends to handle its Premier League challengers. Though I will admit we couldn't get past one team, St Ives. This was mostly because they had a kid who at age nine could somehow perform a scissor kick, the likes of which none of us had ever seen. He, too, must have had a parent from some far-off football-obsessed nation — maybe Brazil or Germany or the Netherlands—who'd instilled a few techniques when there wasn't a lot to be found elsewhere in the competition. Well, we won a lot of games under Dad's determined and sometimes fiery tutelage, but we couldn't quite match this kid, which in hindsight was about as good a lesson as any.

Christmas Glow

What I remember so distinctly about Christmas as a kid was torn wrapping paper all over the living room at 6 a.m. There were a lot of nice things, most of them wrapped in that thin Christmas paper you get at the supermarket typically dotted with Santa faces or little Rudolphs, maybe variously coloured Christmas trees or stars. There was always green and red paper, but sometimes pale blue or white, other times there was silver or gold. All ripped and ruffled, intermittently covering our wooden floorboards like giant confetti pieces, it was our very own festive season parade. A widely tossed spread of wrapping paper usually meant a good session of present opening, where the recipients, us kids, were so jazzed by the size and shape of the gifts and so taken by the process of revealing them, that any mess left around for us to clean up barely registered. We were in the zone, and Christmas morning was always about being in the zone.

It started with an early wake-up call, and being the eldest sibling, I was always the one to initiate it. I'd had strict instructions from Dad to be sure to get everyone up first, my three siblings chiefly, then him and Mum, before rushing out and tearing through the gifts. Of course, I found it hard to wait and most years would creep out into the hallway to steal a peak, imagining I was Skywalker in Cloud City, stealthily moving about as I searched for Darth Vader. On one amazing morning, my brother and I actually received Star Wars blasters, the type Luke and Han yielded in *The Empire Strikes Back*! Well, that Christmas I re-enacted my hallway sneaking with my blaster in hand, after having already crept across the floorboards an hour earlier. I also recall one year both Andy and I received Flash Gordon sets, complete with red Flash singlet and laser guns that lit up and echoed a repetitive beep. We slipped on the singlets without hesitation and began blasting each other across the living room, the six-foot plastic tree in the background at risk of being vapourised should one of our weapons actually unload a real life death ray. It might have happened, who were we to doubt the validity of such things?

Similarly, we revved up the engines of our new remote control cars, off-road vehicles with spiked tyres and lightweight chassis that allowed them to launch well into the air when steered at full speed over an atlas standing in for a jump. There were a lot of different car models sold at the time, many of them high-priced high-speed affairs that were a little bit beyond our expertise. Our parents knew this of course, and wisely picked up the Taiyo Jet Hopper, a Japanese toy that was noticeably slower than the supposedly more high-end Grasshopper, made by another company called Tamiya. The word on the street was that the Grasshopper was the superior vehicle, its red and green stripes across its white body indicating that it was readier for the business of racing than the slightly boxier Jet Hopper, which was also less distinct in red and black. The Jet Hopper also had a spare tyre on the roof, which I loved, but even at nine could understand why my rival racers might consider it a little on the conservative side. Listen, there was nothing safe or even soft about the way my brother and I got the Jet Hopper to move across our paved front yard. That thing flew at a whopping 23 kilometres per hour, speedy enough to shock the dog into a standstill and send the magpies skyward. And yet the roar of a neighbouring Grasshopper was always in the distance, on hand to remind us that it could leave its human remote controller for dust at a scorching 27 km per hour. That was fine, Christmastime wasn't about hitting top speeds, was it? No, it was about hitting that top-of-the-world feeling. It never felt higher than on Christmas morning really, when Mum and Dad would stumble in from a shortened slumber, wondering what we got and if it needed batteries. Then it was hot coffee and Milo, crumpets and panettone. And before a big Christmas lunch with the family, a baked ham, turkey, potato bake, and Dad's famous garlic prawns, we'd fire up the Jet Hopper, see if we could clear a cricket bat, a Chewbacca figurine and three Micro Machines in one jump. It was the time for miracles after all.

Parks and Recreation

On the way to a few holiday spots, we'd pass parks that boasted huge climbing structures shaped like rockets. In my little mind, there were only a couple of these, one west of Sydney near the Blue Mountains and one in the Southern Highlands of New South Wales in Mittagong. But I've since discovered there were many, many more of these rockets stationed around Australia, decorating numerous park spaces and giving tiny track-suited astronauts everywhere a chance to play Marvin the Martian. The rarity of seeing these seven or eight-metre-high red or yellow metal skeleton ships only heightened the experience when you were five. I mean, why were these things available to us to climb anyway? Who put them there? What great mind thought of designing them with multiple floors, joined by a series of ladders, and then thought, we need a slippery dip at the base of these things?

The launch sequence of events is hard to pinpoint here but apparently, it was a Blue Mountains-based engineer who started the builds after a trip to America, at least that's according to a story in a suburban Sydney newspaper called *The Post*. Then these rockets were driven to all sorts of locations in the 1960s, from which point on five-year-olds Australia-wide were begging their parents to pull into 'The Rocket Park' for ten minutes en route to a motel or caravan park somewhere. Little did any of us tikes realise over several decades that we could have climbed multiple rockets in multiple parks—if only we had Google! The rockets were said to mark the space age of the sixties and the world's new fascination with star-bound travel. And yet, surely the market for these wondrous structures couldn't have been bigger than immediately post George Lucas's *Star Wars* movies in the late seventies and early eighties. Only then was the toy technology sufficient enough to have young rocketeers equipped appropriately with cutting-edge laser guns, lightsabers and Han Solo-level courage. I can tell you right now that Andy and I wouldn't have made it beyond the second landing without a two-speed laser pistol made by Kenner.

Fun in a park could also be much louder and wilder, especially when rides were concerned. Some car trips took us by fairs and fetes, carnivals and festivals, and if we were lucky enough Dad would swing the Volvo in for some fairy floss and a few go-rounds on the merry-go-round.

There were other white-knuckle affairs, too, like the Gravitron or Rotor, giant enclosed disc-shaped spinning things that use centrifugal force to stick riders to the walls and help them bring up their lunches. I hated these sorts of rides, never quite seeing the appeal of getting a second taste of my sausage sandwich, though I always felt in the minority on such debates. No big deal, I earned my stripes by braving the rollercoaster and usually many times over. In fact, on a quiet afternoon in Australia's Wonderland in 1988, Andy, John and I rode The Bush Beast twelve times straight! There were no tears, stomach cramps or even a hint of dampness in the underpants. We carried this task out like completing a maths test at school—with equal measures of nonchalance and confusion. You do these sorts of things when you're eleven or twelve, with no eye towards how you might feel afterwards or whether or not a dozen trips on a wooden death-trap might be one too many for the fates to allow. We endured but Wonderland eventually closed its gates, probably after three idiot kids forced The Bush Beast to make thirteen consecutive trips without pause.

Soon enough we were onto other amusement parks such as Dreamworld on Queensland's Gold Coast and Luna Park perched on Sydney's harbourfront. Luna was a short drive away for our family, so we popped in a fair bit during the eighties. Back then there were way more rides, including the dreaded Pirate Ship which swung from side to side like a giant pendulum until all of the change fell from your pockets and your Luna tickets blew away in the breeze. This sort of ride was devised by a madman in my book, the sort of degenerate who got his kicks out of seeing kids come close to barfing, only to have it go back down as his insane contraption swung back from its sickening crescendo. Call me a spoil sport, I don't care, I'd typically have been forced into seven or eight trips round the Love Express prior to manning the Pirate Ship, so you might understand why I wasn't exactly chuffed to ride Luna Park's love boat. I did however love the Dodgems, The Wild Mouse single-car roller coaster and Coney Island with its old-school wooden slides. No day out to Luna Park was ever complete without a few slide burns inside Coney Island capped by some frantic driving on the Dodgems, where Dad could perfect his best road rage lines. It was best that he issued his most choice words from inside a small electric bumper car rather than along the Pacific Highway on the way home, also giving us a better chance of convincing him to pick up some Golden Gaytimes on the way home.

Fizzy Drinks and A Family Size

Crack...pop ... fsssssst...! I'm not sure why I was obsessed with Pepsi as a pre-teen. Yes, it tasted so splendidly sweet to my 11-year-old lips, but something mystical was going on beyond its iconic flavour. I mean I *still* like it more than Coke, and the only thing I can attribute this to is that I was smitten with Pepsi's cultural cache—it's make-believe idealism and commercial schtick. Both the ads Pepsi ran and the ties the company made to cultural superstars played a big role in drawing me in, too. Like the Death Star's tractor beam sucking in the Millennium Falcon, I was rendered a helpless vessel.

Some of the celebrities spruiking Pepsi at the time were Michael Jackson, David Bowie, Madonna, Don Johnson in his *Miami Vice* get-up and yes, my hero, Michael J Fox. Promotional rosters don't come much better than that. The ads were always sexy and upbeat—they were irresistible to kids of all ages because we aspired to be in the very scenes these people were in, to deliver cool throwaway catch phrases as they would and to knock back a soft drink as if to say,

"This is our drink, Mum and Dad—you can park the blackcurrant juice and muesli bars. We've seen the future and its syrupy sweet well branded cola!" Speaking of brands that landed, I was smitten with 7Up too. In fact, I built a tower of 7Up cans in my bedroom in 1987, for what reason I'm unsure. But I loved the green cans, the red dot logo and the animated commercials with that stick figure fellow, Fido Dido. He was almost as cool as Marty McFly throwing down Diet Pepsi at the family dinner table. And while he barely spoke and sauntered around in just two dimensions, his attitude was everything. Once again, the ad people knew what they were doing. Maybe part of my appreciation for these soft drinks came from my devotion to Pizza Hut. It was the best place for pizza-pie where we grew up, but also the perfect spot for a Saturday night dinner with your family, where a buffet of pan-fried pizzas awaited next to a colourful array of sides under a hutted salad bar hood. Our family would roll up to the pizza bar and shovel slices of super supreme, ham and pineapple and plain cheese onto our plates, and then trot giddily back to our booth to deposit the food—merely a holding area as we scrambled back to the drinks dispenser with plastic cups. Crushed ice and plenty of watered-down Pepsi or 7Up awaited at the drinks fountain. Which brilliant marketing flunky came up with this innovative dining programme?

Now I realise that Pizza Hut pizza isn't quite the same as today's authentic Margherita from one of the many Neapolitan-style pizzerias dotted around our cities, but the combo of a heavily topped supreme and cold Pepsi is just unmatched in my mind—even 35 years later. It's tasty and uncomplicated, if not heralded by food reviewers, which is why it's easy to love. Pizza Hut and Pepsi, this easily forgotten dietary favourite of the eighties, was also typically enjoyed at home, delivered just in time for our favourite evening TV shows.

One that we often gathered for was *Married with Children*, much to the chagrin of Mum who wasn't a supporter of Al Bundy and his crude antics. Al's funny lines aside, her harsh feedback makes a lot more sense now, so it was just as well we had other shows to lean on like *Doogie Howser MD, The Wonder Years, The Fall Guy* and *The A-Team*. There were British favourites, too, such as *The Benny Hill Show, Hale and Pace* and *The Two Ronnies*. So many good laughs and a lot of salty dough and sugar-rich cola to go with it. And you thought bingeing was invented by Netflix, shame on you!

I also have fond memories of counting down till 6.30 on Saturday evenings when Australia's most beloved variety show *Hey, Hey It's Saturday* started, which my family marked with a large barbecue chicken, large meat lovers and a large super supreme. Dad would park himself in his usual seat in the corner, Mum on the lighter Scandinavian-style armchair, while we kids perched ourselves on the sofa within arm's reach of the pizza boxes. As Daryl Sommers introduced the Red Faces talent contest and John Blackman took jibes during Molly Meldrum's album reviews, we devoured cheesy pizza and bantered about the weekend's soccer results and which Star Wars film was the best. The weekends were really something to look forward to.

The Mac Pack

The thing about fast food is that it's fun, not just fast. And nobody did it like McDonald's when we were kids, a time when the promotion of its restaurants hotted up like a fresh patty on the grill. McDonald's as we know it started way back in the fifties, sure, but it was really only after a few decades of trade that the company hit worldwide cultural significance. This might be because, at that time, Maccas introduced so many of the items we've come to love since. For example, Chicken McNuggets debuted in '83 and kids went ballistic for them. If that wasn't enough, the company's iconic cardboard lunch pails for littlies launched in 1979, gleefully accepted by the public, always happy for a free gift. The freebies in Happy Meals were generally little plastic toys, often supplied by a partnering brand like Star Wars, Hot Wheels, Muppet Babies or Nintendo's Super Mario Bros.

If you thought McDonald's couldn't top that, in '86 they rolled out Mac Tonight, a moon-headed mascot with dark shades doing his piano rendition of the old Bobby Darin tune, 'Mack the Knife.' Was there ever a catchier jingle from a fast-food chain? Okay, sure, The Black Stump's 'famous for our steaks' diddy was pretty strong, too. On a more superficial level, if that's possible, Maccas did some of the best branded goodies I can recall, from Snoopy and Garfield drinking glasses to plastic Flintstones cups and even McDonald's character pens. Most of this stuff was unnecessary but it just made the experience of eating the food more thrilling. I mean, what other eateries were matching the Golden Arches on brand association? Very few and, in fact, so impactful was the collecting of such items, that you can ask anyone who was a child at the time and they'll smile reminiscently.

I understand the frivolity of this in 2024, but it was a different time and the over consumption of useless goods and environmental issues were hardly top of mind. Indeed, the accumulation of commercial curiosities designed to clutter cupboards was. We see this acutely when we think back to Styrofoam boxes. I'm sorry, but the old boxes looked great, especially the bright yellow one with red lettering atop it indicating that the contents within were my delicious Quarter Pounder. It was usually kept warm in the car by sitting under the Big Mac and Filet-O-Fish Dad would include in the family order. We'd all then unpack our boxes from those iconic white paper bags and settle in for a film, maybe even an evening of Monopoly or a card game. Sundays were almost as good as Saturdays and McDonald's helped create that connection for many families, as trivial as that may sound. Yes, nostalgia overrides common sense in these sorts of matters, but that's just the way memory works. Like the regular toy offerings, the highly 'ungreen' packaging of the eighties was for a limited time only, and that was for the best.

For me, the memory will always be tied to my dad especially. Dad quite possibly had too much fast food in the eighties because that sort of stuff caught up to him a bit later on. But still, I don't think he would have regretted all the fun times we had around our take away family meals. I relished those car trips with him to McDonald's after a win at our morning soccer match, or indeed to collect the family's dinner early Sunday evening. These were times for us to chat about an old John Wayne movie he just rewatched for the fifty-ninth time, or to blow up together because the ref missed a call late in a Norths-Souths game, or maybe he'd share with us his views on the most recent Eurovision Song Contest and why the Swedes or the Greeks or whoever deserved the gong. We might have even discussed the Maccas menu, tackling the common contention that a Quarter Pounder was better than a McFeast. Now that was an unanswerable question for the ages, and yet perfect for the twelve minute drive over to the Golden Arches.

Cartoonish

The beauty of printed comic books was that you could stack them high in a box, a drawer or atop your desk—piled ready for a flick-through at all times. Many of us adore the always-accessible content on smartphones in the same way. I don't hate my smartphone, nor am I against finding entertainment on it, but I really did enjoy collecting physical comic books as a kid, each a storybook and showcase of art that offered the tactility of art within a typically glossy cover. All the artists and writers were listed within, and I enjoyed reading those too as if each book was made just for me or my brother or sis. That they'd grow musty and yellow was never really a problem because the ageing of comic books, and indeed printed books, always felt like part of the lifecycle to me. Art ages as if alive, that's what I've always thought. In the digital world, it feels like everything is part of the current time, always accessible and instantly referenced. In other words, it just doesn't seem to age. It's timeless in every sense of the word.

It's terrific that today you can always find a digitally produced comic and that the creators of them have a forum to produce such material, but to me, the comic or cartoon art of the eighties will always feel closer to the actual hand or mind of the illustrator. I mean anyone who loves Charlie Brown knows the poor little bloke isn't a high-def, hyper-colour sort of fellow! I guess the other part is that comic book shops are so uncommon now that you're largely locked into the digital version. The experience of dawdling through those venues as a kid in Sydney's CBD is something that I look back on rather fondly. Comic Kingdom is the one that comes to mind, a pretty low fuss, well-trodden establishment filled to the edges with books old and new, plus posters, toys, trinkets and collectables. I remember rushing upstairs to grab a new edition of *Spiderman* or *Wolverine* and having the uptight hawkeyed manager watch our every move. I guess I would have done the same. After all, this was his museum, to take the art analogy further. The hawkeyed manager wouldn't give us 30 seconds to browse the latest edition of *Hawkeye* because he thought we had grubby hands and too cool attitudes perhaps. Maybe we did, but we also had $10 worth of pocket money each, so you know, we were his most loyal customers and willing to spend.

Comics were sold at lots of places in the eighties. At the local newsagent in Lindfield, Dad would lead us to the comic shelves at the back where *Phantom*, *Batman* and other comic classics like *Archie* and *Scooby Doo* awaited, but that was just half of it. Comic strip books like Murray Ball's *Footrot Flats* were also on hand, boasting superbly playful covers bounding beautifully drawn black and white strips. The shop also had these illustrated cardboard scenes that came complete with etching sheets of characters and objects that you could scratch onto the crisp backdrop with a pen. You placed these things wherever you wanted, a revelation to my eight-year-old self.

I recall joyfully scribbling the *Dukes of Hazzard* car into the sky of a country scene, as if airborne above a hill and a river, you know, the way the Duke boys typically were in every single episode. Except here, I could position the trajectory of the car however I best imagined it, often above an oak or even a barn—something I doubt the Dukes actually achieved, even in the souped-up General Lee! Dad loved the classics, too, the sort of comic strips that would appear in the daily newspaper such as *The Sun* or *The Daily Mirror*. We all liked them: Archie, Fred Basset, Snake, Ginger Meggs, Hagar, The Wizard of Id, Peanuts, B.C, Andy Capp, Zits, The Phantom, Prince Valiant and of course, Garfield. I think Dad possibly preferred older ones from his childhood, but I always had the sense that if it was drawn, boxed and speech-bubbled, he'd give it a go, even more than the general news, but maybe not more than the sports pages. Undoubtedly his favourite periodical was the Italian magazine, *La Settimana Enigmistica*, a mostly black and white puzzle filled publication with crosswords, spot-the-difference contests, gags, word games and general knowledge questions. A copy of the magazine would typically lay at his bedside at all times, creased or crumpled, snug beneath a packet of Fisherman's Friends throat lozenges, a pile of loose change and a book on World War II ships or Aesop's Fables. It's funny how fathers collect things and even funnier that we notice the smorgasbord of oddities.

For me and my brother, the magazine by our bedsides was *Mad*, the legendary humour rag of cartoon parodies and punch lines, movie spoofs and pop culture cuts, that for any kid of the eighties was required reading. The mag started in the 1950s, but it could be argued really found its groove in the seventies and eighties when movies and music took bigger leaps and darker turns, celebrities presented themselves as overly important to the culture and TV expanded well beyond standard family units and wholesome community ideals.

Subsequently, the gag-masters at Mad were ready to pounce. We loved it, stockpiling our editions with the dedication of an aluminium-hatted hoarder ahead of a hit by Halley's Comet, like the one that some certainly expected in 1986. Mad had it all in the way of comedy, and much of the sensibility for humour was guided by the writers and artists at the magazine, who were like the funny kid at the back of the class, wacky, irreverent and faster than the teacher. When they made fun of blockbuster films like *Die Hard*, *Field Of Dreams* and *Caddyshack*, we loved the upending of such pop culture staples.

And when they revised the lyrics of a pop song from Micheal Jackson or Madonna, we felt like the correction was warranted even though we loved the original artefacts in equal measure. That was the brilliance of Mad's satire, which the colour and pomp of the eighties was ripe for, and which pop culture-saturated little minds seemed perfectly made to absorb.

Easter Goodies

One event we loved growing up was the Easter Show, where Dad, Andy and I covered more miles than Rob de Castella and uncovered more junk food than Fat Albert (that was a real TV show, please don't write in!). It was at Moore Park back then, at the aptly named Showgrounds.

The whole thing was geared around this inner city space and, as such, it always felt like an escape to a fantastical land across the harbour, completely removed from our everyday suburban life. Since the 'Show' has moved to the Homebush Olympic grounds in the west of Sydney, it hasn't felt as special to me. I'm sure this opinion resonates with anyone who recalls the old show because it's simply a change.

One thing hasn't changed and that's the magnetic allure of show bags, those wonderfully commercially marked and jam-packed bags of goodies nobody needs but every kid wants. The entire show visit centred around acquiring bags and as many of them as possible. My brother and I tagged along with Dad to various displays and pavilions, enduring crusty old guys spruiking useless knick-knacks and Dagwood dogs, mostly because we needed time to dream about which bags we'd line up for. Back then, the prices were ludicrously low, too, and so the idea of scoring six or seven bags each was not out of the question. Some years the haul was modest, but there were others in which I know we possibly broke records for the number of show bags picked up in the five to seven-year-old category. Three in each hand was standard unless you were overly eager and took on a typically bulky bag like those offered to fans of *M.A.S.H, The A-Team* or *Knight Rider*. Good gear if you could handle the extra baggage. But we were mostly obsessed with smaller treats. The best part of getting bags full of salty and powder-dusted chips, bubbly soft drinks and useless plastic items like twirl-shaped straws, oversized sports caps and crappy wallets made with questionable-grade velcro, was stashing them under our beds like pirates hoarding treasure. This stuff was our annual loot, very unhealthy food, and unsanctioned and poorly designed plastic goods, which remained in their plastic bags in our rooms for weeks on end. We simply scooped up a treat as needed, in between rounds of Metroid on the Nintendo. What an era!

In all seriousness though, I truly loved having mini mountains of chips and soft drinks buried under my bed. It was more fun than just about anything I can recall from the time, perhaps other than winning a weekend soccer game by ten goals or completing a stage of Super Mario Brothers in record-breaking fashion. But ultimately scoring this stash of goodies is such a rich memory because it was shared with my family.

The Easter Show for me was about spending time with my dad and brother, and then showcasing what we picked up for everyone to share at day's end. My dad was such a generous spender and an avid shopper, so entering the Showbag Pavilion was undoubtedly a thrill for him as it was for us. I think he enjoyed the challenge of it all, navigating the bag stands, finding the best ones, and pleasing his kids. He'd busily scan the crowded barn, absorbing the signs and posters decorating each booth in split seconds, always scouring the room for the best deals but mostly spotting the brands he knew his boys favoured: Violet Crumble, Coca-Cola, Milky Way, 7Up, Smiths, CCs, Hubba Bubba, Lifesavers, Sunny Boy and Cadbury, to name just a few. If I think back to our pantry at home, it was filled to the edges with these same brands and many more. The taste for these goodies was well ingrained and so while, we inordinately pined for Easter Show bags of chips, chocolate bars and cans of lemonade, it was more in the vain of a connoisseur, not a glutton. Pirate connoisseurs, if you will.

And so we'd leave the Pavilion weary, hands and arms weighty, feet sore, and yet still buoyed by the sheer thrill of it all. We'd pile into Dad's old blue Volvo, sacks of treats strewn across the back seat, and listen to the footy on the radio all the way home, while munching through some cheesy puff balls, followed by a shot or two of cola. Could it ever get any better than that? Later on, Dad would tell Mum about the brilliant display of vegetables in one of the farming warehouses, or some of the great animals we saw, cows, horses and pigs. He might have even described the wood-chopping competition. But I'm pretty sure he skipped over the rest...the greasy lunch of hot dogs and pies, the highly impractical novelty toys we collected—whoopee cushions, rubber spiders and inflatable baseball bats, and maybe the high cost of multiple Slushies...it all went straight to our bedrooms, both the knick-knacks and memories, our Easter treasure chests always topped full.

Popcorn Flicks

In 1985, movies were rather original, often very funny, brash, sometimes loud, and presented striking heroes and heroines that people wanted to be as much as watch. For example, we walked out of Roseville Cinema after *Raiders Of The Lost Ark* on a spring afternoon in 1981, not only thrilled by the story but convinced that we now needed to smirk in the face of danger, crack a mean whip and most importantly, search for lost ancient religious artefacts. Short of genuine archaeological sites, my brother and I excavated old Star Wars figurines from the soil in the backyard, typically unearthing a less coveted character such as IG-88 or one of the Sandpeople.

More valuable treasures were certainly available, say the Matchbox jeep from the Fall Guy TV show or even a rare Smurf figure, Jokey or Smurfette perhaps. Sure, there were no giant boulders or poison darts to ruin our day, but our house was bordered by a creek at the back, so there were plenty of mosquitoes I assure you. Soon after, *The Goonies* reinforced such ideas because the heroes were our own age and a little less grizzled. But both movies were effective motivators for eighties kids, weaving together action, comedy and fantasy on the Village and Hoyts big screens in about two hours. And if the stunts and spooky scenes didn't grab you, then a moving and often award-winning musical score would.

They like to talk about movie magic in Hollywood, and I don't think the spell was ever more potent than when the era's great filmmakers like Steven Spielberg went to work, teamed up with cutting-edge special effects people and asked John Williams and his orchestra to come up with a little diddy. These great creators presented us with the perfect experience for consuming huge quantities of popcorn and soft drink, Skittles and Choc Tops, perhaps more than any time before it and certainly ever since. Of course, my point of view on all this is skewed by the sugar rush of too many Gummy Bears and through rose-tinted 3D glasses. But if you can think of a movie in the last twenty years outside of a Harry Potter flick that lives up to the sense of spirited adventure in *The Goonies*, well, I'll happily do the Truffle Shuffle for you! But what was different back then that saw these sorts of films made so regularly? Why were these zany ideas heralded as blockbuster material, when now it feels like the only thing that qualifies is to see someone in padded tights tossing some poor schmuck through a computer-generated wall?

Maybe a good film to consider here, and yet another that wouldn't get over the line in 2024, is 1986's *Big Trouble In Little China*. We loved this flick in my house, mostly because it starred Kurt Russell as the wise-cracking-tough-guy truckie, but also because it blended frantic action, manic martial arts, ludicrous weaponry, sorcery, violence, soft horror and even a bit of romance. This tale had it all—including levitating bad guys, creepy monsters and plucky female leads—and yet it offered very little cohesion. It was loud, funny and downright loopy! Only a filmmaker like John Carpenter in an era when studios were loose with their cash could produce such a masterpiece of popcorn culture.

Indeed, many of the memorable movies we grew up with had some element of the enigmatic, rebellious or odd—

Predator, Stripes, The Lost Boys, Gremlins, Fletch, The Breakfast Club, Romancing the Stone, Escape From New York, 48 Hours, Ferris Bueller's Day Off, Ghostbusters, Terminator, Caddyshack, Commando and *The Princess Bride*, to name just a few. The typically oddball premises of these might seem strange in retrospect and yet, one might say they were clever, artistic or at the very least, riskier concepts and narratives than the norm. Yes, in some instances the plots were pretty thin, but a dedication to characters typically won moviegoers over. How else can we explain the success of a film like *The Breakfast Club*? Like bad boy John Bender, the eighties movie honchos apparently didn't care about what people thought. They just did their thing and that was very cool.

Weekends weren't limited to the theatre because wall-to-wall VHS and Beta tapes at the video store were just a short drive away. We had a couple of options in our local area, but the one I recall most fondly was a hole-in-the-wall two suburbs over called Tri-Star Video. Run by a slightly overweight and unshaven video savant named Tony, Tri-Star was the ideal place for young moviegoers looking for an obscure teen-level title with screwball themes, light swearing and gratuitous poolside romping. We'd often call Tony in advance just to hear his deadpan and nasally delivery about a movie release, and in a typically uninspired way, Tony would give us the scoop better than Margaret Pomeranz of *The Movie Show*! Tri-Star didn't boast rows of the latest releases starring Schwarzenegger or Stallone, but rather, offered the more adventurous video hunter a B-grade special—a low-budget comedy vehicle for an eighties up-and-comer like John Cusack, Rob Lowe and the one and only, Michael J Fox.

Fox featured in many 1980s B-graders, including *High School USA, Poison Ivy* and *Teen Wolf. The Secret of My Success* and *Bright Lights, Big City* soon followed. But even with all those small screen beauties to his name, it was his contemporary Cusack that perhaps owned the day, at least as far as filling the shelves of Tri-Star. Some of Johnny C's best-known hits—typically stowed away in the comedy section at most shops—were easy to find in the front half of the Tri-Star emporium, because that's just how Tony rolled.

Among them were cult hits *Better Off Dead* and *Say Anything*. But real Cusack aficionados like us preferred an even deeper dive into the Tri-Star galaxy, where we might just plunge into a black hole of underappreciated eighties goofball classics. Two of our favourites were *One Crazy Summer* and *Hot Pursuit*, while others such as *The Sure Thing* and *Class* were sufficient back-ups, should those films have been labelled 'Out' or 'Due Back Next Week.' Of course, Tony's five tapes for $7 deal was also an option, should we be unable to decide. Though that was always a risky endeavour because we'd inevitably take weeks to get through all five movies, resulting in a tidy tally of late fees that even our mate Tony couldn't overlook. *Hot Pursuit* holds a special place in my heart because I recall watching it with my brother, Andy after we ambitiously ordered a footlong super supreme from Pizza Hut with a huge bottle of Pepsi. Mum and Dad had gone out to see some friends, so we convinced them to let us stay home, pig out and yes, choose our own movie. This is surely the pinnacle of the childhood experience.

I distinctly remember the superb video cover of *Hot Pursuit* demanding our attention, its sexy rendering of a blonde bombshell spying on the hopelessly lost teenage protagonist Cusack through a pair of binoculars. The cover alone was part of the allure, telling us back in the cosy confines of Tri-Star that this was the film to babysit even the most restless pre-adolescents on any given Saturday night. Well, we loved the highly flawed Cusack fiasco, and we feebly finished the footlong, too.

In the end, we were left sprawling on the sofa, satisfied by senseless screwball slapstick and strongly spiced salami. What a night!

I think these types of memories owe a lot to the humble video store. Before the Netflix era, these movie havens were the primary go-to for home entertainment but also brought about a community feeling that came with physically browsing the store. Unlike streaming the latest flicks from your couch, such places actually required you to front up in your tracksuit pants and Dorito-stained t-shirt to actually walk the aisles in person. Other people were there, too, can you believe it? This interaction was indeed part of the experience, both competing with people in your neighbourhood for a limited supply of movies and also sharing the moment with them as you passed each other trying to find the perfect film. Listen, there was a chance you might miss out. There was also a high probability that following the crowd inside the store could lead you astray. You might also run into a family friend, someone keener on a chat than spotting a copy of Tom Cruise's latest feature. Hey, great to see you, Stevo, but step aside pal, we've got a date with The Cruiser sliding across the floor to Old Time Rock and Roll!

Just as we loved taking Mum and Dad's old records off the shelf, so too did we revel in sampling movie tapes off the shelves. I think the enjoyment of borrowing them was that they were tangible items, not merely streamed over Wi-Fi networks. Picking up a video cover and studying it at the store truly required focus—at least more than that needed for scrolling through apps while lounging around in your underpants! Let's not pull punches, gang. Decisions were made promptly in the eighties video store, good and bad, because there was a pizza on its way and everyone in the family wanted to settle in quick smart. This was a totally different experience to today's movie choosing process within bottomless content libraries.

Personally, I miss the gamble of the video store, the immediacy of the transaction of paying the rental fee on a movie that might be a real bomb. That can't happen now. On top of this, all of today's online discussion and constant assessment of movies makes it impossible to make a choice of your very own. The choices—the popular ones—are pretty much already known. This was not the experience of going to Blockbuster, Video Ezy, or the great, Tri-Star Video. We entered those sacred arenas as if it were Thunderdome, Mel Gibson-style mullets and Tina Turner manes preened for the dangers of perusing.

Joysticks and Buttons

Once we polished off our favourite treats and got through the movies, there were games. As the Netflix folks have well documented, our childhoods coincided with the wellspring of video game culture. But what was it about those simple eight-bit games that drew kids, exactly? The newness of the technology was certainly part of it, navigating imagined digital worlds with sprightly sprites and upbeat theme songs. It was escapism and storytelling, but also compelling and compulsive adventures that seemed to eclipse books, comics ...and even films. At the centre of the gaming story, the slightly more evolved era that eclipsed say, Atari, was the original Nintendo. The little grey box with a red logo, ready to ingest plastic cartridge games, quickly became the focus of our living room, and indeed the true obsession of kids the world over.

Initially, it was those plumbing Mario Brothers that we targeted, but soon enough our game draws were filled with many titles such as Kid Icarus, Metroid, Mega Man, Metal Gear, Rad Racer, Castlevania, Ice Hockey and Double Dribble. Loads of games followed, of course, though it wasn't really about how many games you had, but rather, for how long you could sink into the titles you had. One of the great time-suckers was 'Zelda' a fantasy adventure long before those gurus at Gryffindor were conjured in which magic, swords, monsters and wizards scored incredibly well with nine-year-olds, where they could collect little digitised gems that let them buy weapons and potions. But the game was pretty damn challenging and took hours of commitment, along with an endless supply of Arnott's Monte chocolate biscuits.

Incidentally, Monte eventually took a backseat to the much-hyped Tim Tam, but we never wavered from them. They fuelled our many Nintendo sessions, lengthy pixel-pumping stints that perfectly broke up an afternoon of shooting hoops in the yard. Indeed, summer Nintendo matches were epic, mostly because they were the ideal way to sit inside with the curtain drawn to escape the heat!

Of course, Nintendo continues its success today and so this distant past feels very present and connected to the games kids play today. Nintendo cleverly plays on this nostalgic memory, too, ensuring that many of its latest games are iterations of these original titles. Outside of underpants and ice cream trucks, there aren't many things in popular culture that boast such a seamless continuum. I mean this little wonder of Japanese innovation is still with us in one form or another, and even if you don't have a new version, chances are there's an old dusty model tucked away in one of your cupboards.

Unlike many toys, this thing remains both in our mind's eye and sitting in the middle of our 2024 homes. We have both an artefact and a new invention, an ongoing thread of the familiar and new, and something that joins the generations. My point is I don't think this continuity is something my parents could really ever enjoy. They played us Beatles and Beach Boys records, sure, and certainly, we had a moment with toys they too used like frisbees, marbles and slingshots.

But any connection we had to their youth was limited or perhaps overridden by a new phase of technological and computer-enhanced toys. We were totally engrossed in them and dare I say distracted, too. I like to think the 'Game Over' after each Nintendo contest urged us to turn them off for a while. But that just might be wishful thinking—we probably played for hours on end just as kids today settle in for Roblox or Minecraft on their screens. Still, those old games were far less interactive and immersive, so it was unlikely that you'd ever be wholly absorbed by the eight-bit graphics and simpler storylines. I mean they were never all that realistic. Can you imagine, though? What I would have given to be shrunk down like Mike TV in *Charlie and The Chocolate Factory* and then reduced to blocky bits to fight alongside Mario and Luigi.

It all started in the arcade. Arcade game centres were a big deal in the US at first, but it wasn't long before companies like Timezone jumped into the fray, offering Aussies coin-operated game units in popular shopping areas. What stands out about this early gaming period is that there wasn't a lot on offer otherwise—I mean places for kids and teenagers to gather and enjoy an activity together. I guess Mum and Dad could have booked you into a holiday camp, where maybe you learned a bit of acting or singing, had a tennis lesson or kicked a ball around. But the only other place where you might have run amok was any place that offered video game cabinets. If you were lucky, one or two gaming machines could typically be found in corner shop milk bars, pizzerias and even the entertainment rumpus room of a hotel. I recall being very excited about the prospect that a wooden box standing in the corner of some old shop might boast the circuit boards of Zaxxon or Asteroids within.

Indeed, some of the holiday accommodations we frequented housed such marvellous things. Similarly, a burger shop by the beach might have had a pinball machine in its farthest corner so that instead of aimlessly scrolling through a smartphone while waiting for a cheeseburger, you could pop a couple of twenty-cent coins in and play the Six Million Dollar Man or Star Trek in a glorious pinballing format. For us, that initial gaming place wasn't actually an arcade or a hotel but a bowling alley not far from our home. While we adored the little yellow gobbling pizza face Pac-Man, as well as the manic jumping frog trying to get across the road named Frogger, it was an American football game that most grabbed our attention, 10-Yard Fight. Sports and video games are perhaps a natural pairing. They both elicit feelings of passion, commitment, delight and despair. They are competition, albeit on different planes. And they require a special type of nutty fanaticism to see a game through.

Over the years, sports-themed games have really made their mark and titles like Madden (American football), FIFA Soccer, Tiger Woods Golf, NBA 2K (basketball) and even Mario Kart are typically at the top of favourite game lists. And these don't include all the retro greats like Mike Tyson's Punch-Out, California Games or Jordan Vs Bird: One on one; we loved all of these titles in my family and each captivated us in its own way, but few made a lasting impression like 10-Yard Fight. Yes, it was a simplistic side-scrolling affair, limited by early-era sixteen-bit graphics and in its rudimentary game play. But it was nonetheless advanced for 1985, and as close to playing NFL quarterback as we imagined we'd ever get. I was nine when it was released, which also gifted me with a suitable lack of expectation and a necessary amount of patience to enjoy such a simplistic game.

To be fair, these sorts of games didn't lack charm. What 10-Yard Fight had in its favour—as anyone nostalgic about the original batch of Nintendo offerings will attest to—was a very straightforward concept. No fancy intro featuring Kid Rock or Creed here. No verbose broadcaster snippets on a loop. No overcompensating mini-games filling out the main menu, which can typically happen when a product is bogged down by complex playbooks. Instead, 'Fight' focused on single-minded fun and to do so, it offered just one attacking mode—the read option. As is the case in real American football, your quarterback simply took the snap and could make one of three choices: 1) run, 2) toss the ball horizontally to a running back, or 3) throw the ball to a lone downfield receiver. It was the sort of stark, unscheduled, draw-it-up-in-the-sand approach to football that made you fall in love with the hero of every high school football movie out of Hollywood.

And here it was in pink and blue pixels. Fight's central playmaker hurriedly scanned for space, read the lean of defenders' bodies and chose an angle, by foot or by air. To me, it was a single premise, but with an understated beauty brought about only by its uncomplicated narrative. And despite all this, 10-Yard Fight is still polarising because most gamers, and even those with a penchant for anything retro, prefer the oft-heralded Tecmo Bowl. And to be fair, Tecmo is a superb blend of dynamism and graphical prowess in hindsight. Tecmo deserves its ongoing appreciation. Fight never matched its gameplay. And yet it made up the difference with quirky, old fashioned touches, chief of which were its sound effects.

The way I see it, football deconstructed into 10-Yard struggles posed a feasible and enticing challenge, kind of like the 'It' girls they cast in the aforementioned teen movies: Cindy Mancini in Can't Buy Me Love or Andy in The Goonies were just the types of love interests nerds locked in their rooms with Nintendo could not attain, but hoped to. So, you see, this little game had its own sort of sex appeal.

But as I look back, I wonder, where did the love of a distinctly American game come from? Seeds were planted early, I guess. When I was about five, Andy and I caught a glimpse of the gridiron on TV. It seemed a weird gladiatorial-looking game in which the players wore metallic helmets and inflated shoulder pads. It looked as though they could do anything in that gear, crash headlong into a pile of granite slabs or launch over a row of Cadillacs. In a sense they did! Soon after we were at the home of family friends, who had just returned from an American vacation, a less common occurrence in the early eighties.

Our pals, Danny and Timmy, told us about what they'd seen of this fantastic game and pointed to a couple of flashy posters they had on their bedroom wall as they did so. My memory of those posters was that they represented two teams—the Dallas Cowboys and the Washington Redskins. What was great about this introduction was that these just so happened to be two of the NFL's most iconic clubs from two very iconic cities. I'm also quite sure that when it came to the helmets worn on the American gridiron field, none were as intriguing or as memorable to the five-year-old's mind than the blue star on a silver background of Dallas, or the native

American face on the crimson red background of Washington. It all came alive when the family showed us a VHS tape of some of the action, and while the details are sketchy in memory, I can recall a Dallas back—probably the Cowboys All-Pro, Tony Dorsett—tearing through the backfield of some schmuck outfit. It was a whirling blur of motion on that tape, colour and pomp like we'd never seen, certainly not in telecasts of our local footy games. The ball rocketing from the arm of a quarterback behind a mass of humanity, spiralling up into the air and beautifully down again into the outstretched arms of a teammate racing downfield was pretty captivating, and so many of the plays were filled with such acrobatics as if the whole sport was designed to have you jumping up from your bean bag every thirty seconds.

Later on, we'd get into a whole selection of teams—the Raiders, Bears, Jets and Broncos but also one with more exotic nicknames like the 49ers, Bengals, Chargers, Dolphins and Giants. It was like football from another planet! What the hell was a 49er, anyway? We'd scan highlight reels aired on Channel 10 after the 8.30 movie. Dad could see we were mad about the game and was good enough to buy a fresh batch of VHS tapes to record weekly games and recaps for us. It was thrilling stuff, the kind of thing that you wanted to re-enact in the hallway.

Soon enough, we imagined hitting the pitch, stuffing socks and underwear under our pyjamas and buckling up our plastic police and fireman helmets, we'd go to gridiron war on Mum's favourite stretch of the floorboard. Tumbling around like Pro Bowlers, we broke all records for family home touchdowns, as well as broken vases.

Buried Treasure

Our young years were also marked by some iconic pop culture products. Why they all came at once I don't know, but there were a lot of light bulb moments apparently, new ideas being tried and money people with brick-sized mobile phones seemed happy to back them. I'm talking left-field, better erased from the board sort of pitches—those allowed to breathe by marketing people who were presumably high on Pop Rocks and Push Pops. How else can we account for so many teen movies with plotlines thinner than the nerdy kid at the heart of them, or portable music players, fluorescent Lycra clothing, ostentatious sports cars with spaceship doors, calculator watches, endless lines of sneakers, cartoon-themed cereals, blockbuster releases about ghosts, gremlins and goons, or mutant turtle and transforming vehicles on toy shelves? Truly, that's just a snapshot of what went on and in itself is zanier than a sketch on Letterman featuring grown men in bear suits, also an eighties staple.

Our memories of the time are a little blurry, of course, and sometimes tinged with glimmering rose-coloured light. In other words, if you were in a happy home where you could enjoy a local corner store, or had a favourite local park where you could pretend to be Diego Maradona or Katarina Witt, and where you could pop a can of TAB with your pals and munch your way through a Space Food bar, then things were pretty good relatively speaking and the thought of it all gives you warm memories today. There's no way to speak for everyone on this, I'm just pointing to the fact that very generally, in an average household, the eighties offered a range of pop culture delights—trivialities of modern life that both consumed and entertained us. They were fairly innocent and innocuous additives to the culture tapestry woven over many decades, but they were also supersonically-charged compared to the machinations of an earlier time.

Three decades after the Second World War, and with mass suburbanisation and consumption well and truly set in, kids of our generation were kind of allowed to be kids. We were perhaps part of a pretty frivolous time in that regard, but I'm thankful and count it as rather fortunate because, in those places that were free of conflict or social upheaval, or other issues of crime and so on, we could both kick a ball outside and retreat inside to man a digital skateboarder flipping across a screen. In 1985, we were front and centre in the cultural mix, ready and waiting to absorb whatever Nerf item or similar could be tossed our way. I mean I think back to some of those plastic figurines that might still be in the ground of our Lindfield home actually, lodged under some rocks, well-trodden soil and even some wild overgrowth these many moons later. Why did we love them so much? They were tiny replicas, often with rigid limbs and limited functionality. And yet they meant so much. So much so that we buried them like treasure!

Those poor guys never stood a chance with a deep jungle of a backyard like ours. Even if over time, the elements dislodged one of Darth Vader's troops from the soil, chances are a magpie would swoop it up and redeposit it in the creek running behind our house. We'd wade through that creek during many summers, undeterred by leeches and washed-up KB beer cans, and hopeful to fish out a relic of an earlier generation—perhaps a lost marble or sunken cricket ball. I guess we did a lot of the same stuff, the way kids always have. Like indulging in good old fashioned make believe, but with the added advantage of new and incredible play things, from He-Man, G I Joe and Optimus Prime to high-speed radio control cars that hit about 25 miles per hour. From handheld video games featuring Donkey Kong and Mickey Mouse to other electronic games like Simon and Speak and Spell. And don't forget those cuddly bears with mechanics inside that made them talk, nor the plastic bedtime worms that glowed in the dark. How did they do that, exactly? There were Pogoballs and laser tag guns, too, Segas and Ataris, Alf and ET dolls, Barbie's pink corvette and pet ponies with beautifully coloured mains. It was playtime on juice!

Even the colours and tones were a bit more fun—removed from the sometimes drab and boho-style seventies, where haircuts outside of the Jackson 5 had little shape. There was a genuine feeling of newness and brightness, and yet it all felt appropriate, on balance. When I look back at family photos from the time, I can't help but smile because it was different, and yet is still so very tangible in the present. Oh, and we had the needlessly triangular-shaped Sunny Boy ice block, so you know, it's hard to deny that it all made for a very special time indeed. But if I'm honest, some of the brightness is related to where we discovered these treasures. For us, it was often inside Uncle Pete's Toys, a wondrous cavern of wall-to-wall goods in nearby St Leonards, where even a tiny kid had to manoeuvre like Franz Beckenbauer through its tightly arranged aisles. And because the shop was close to our home, it meant we always had a chance to beg Dad to swing by and check out the latest Star Wars gear within. Though there was more to it—the aura around Pete's shops was so vibrant and playful that it truly pulled kids towards it like a mystical beacon. This was, in part, due to the lively ads for the shop that featured a kindly old guy who we all assumed was indeed an uncle named Pete.

Uncle Pete would cheerfully spruik his wares to the camera, talk excitedly about newly imported gear, tell us the prices and even jump in to show how some items worked. I recall him once riding a tricycle, which only suggested to me that the bloke loved toys! On occasion, the camera would even pan the shelves, offering just a snippet of the selection Pete had procured, tantalising our appetites for absolutely anything with kooky sounds or mechanical movements. It was magical and I suppose that's why the business ran with the catch cry at the end of every commercial that announced "Uncle Pete's toys are magic!" To our eyes they were.

There was also no shortage of cultural cache in the garbage—if you had Garbage Pail Kids cards that is. Yes, Mum and Dad didn't rate them on any level, not for their witty play on words, hilarious cartoons, or their clever send-up of the overhyped Cabbage Patch Kids. Still, we loved them and couldn't peel the stickers from their cardboard backs any faster to plaster all over notebooks and bed heads, on the leg of a table or random drawer somewhere in the house. The wacky and often very gross series was produced by the Topps company and originally released in 1985 with a satirical tone, but I think quickly transitioned into a higher art form than mere parody. This was clever stuff, boasting such famed caricatures as Jay Decay, Stormy Heather, Adam Bomb and

Bloody Mary. I probably don't need to explain the cartoons, you get the gist.

Anyway, these little guys and gals were more common in the US, where the standard five-pack came with a pretty dry stick of gum for 25c. In Sydney, during the eighties, we paid considerably more. A local novelty shop near our home stocked them and I think we may have been the only customers asking after them at the time. We'd load up on as many packets as possible and also request some other hard to find American staples such as Big League Chew, Wonka Gobstoppers and Hershey's chocolate bars, most of which weren't available in local corner shops as they are now, and subsequently cost us weeks' worth of mowing lawns or running paper routes. Any chore was worth it for a slice of novelty.

Unreal Stories

The books in our house were often classics because Mum was an English teacher. There were the usual heavy affairs from the likes of Charlotte Bronte, Jonathan Swift or Arthur Miller. And we certainly had some Shakespeare collections, the works of Banjo Patterson and the requisite copy of Catch-22. The Bible, of course, and a few different dictionaries. Dad was also partial to a story about mythology, so there was plenty of that sort of thing lying about—flying horses, sea monsters, and one-eyed giants in ill-fitted sandals. There was a very long row of leather-bound encyclopaedias filling a couple of shelves in the front room, too. Oh, and some glossy photography books, many of which had seldom seen pages that were crisper than a McDonald's French fry. The point being that good books were in the house and we hoped to one day be decent little readers like our parents.

That said, there were few books that really inspired us in the early going, well at least nothing that lacked an appearance by either Snoopy or Garfield. That's why nothing prepared me for the excitement I felt upon encountering Paul Jennings' wacky short stories. The bloke had a great knack for the quirky and weird, for the sorts of stories you imagined you might write after bingeing on M&Ms and Wizz Fizz. But really, these were the types of yarns you wanted to pen at school the next time your teacher asked for some 'creative writing.' And indeed I tried, typically churning out some ludicrous tale in which the protagonist found himself in an upside-down world, with green rain and blue trees, his head on backwards and where the people spoke like Jabberjaw. Ultimately, my short story hero would awaken to realise it was all a dream, an ending that I thought was rather clever and completely original.

Thankfully, Paul Jennings was on hand to show us how a tale should go, often taking the everyday experiences of a family, group of friends, or kids in the schoolyard and twisting the circumstances ever so slightly. He perfected the potential uneasiness of our immediate world and that's what resonated. It was his first book 'Unreal' that hit bookstores in June of '85 which first introduced me to this way of storytelling. I was wowed by such classics as *Wunderpants*, *Skeleton on the Dunny* and *Cowdung Custard*—the titles alone evoked a sense of fun and even mystery. And then there were the covers of Jenning's books, typically a random mash of imagery, with creepy faces and set amid some off-putting colours. Some covers looked like the artist Pro Hart had downed a few too many West Coast Coolers. Unreal's cover was as strange as any of them, a blur of green, blue, pink and yellow paint strokes surrounding a smattering of out-of-proportion renderings—a boy's face, a large saxophone, a much smaller clarinet and then a tiny lighthouse in the background. It was bloody eerie and yet wonderful, completely representative of the stories within. Though if I'm honest, this cover especially looked like it might have been snuck past the publisher's desk en route to the final print run. I say all this with undying adoration because it's quite possibly the cover I would have sketched for my own short storybook.

The joy of reading a book aimed squarely at your age group was almost matched by the anticipation of actually obtaining it, and for school kids in the mid-eighties, there were few better shopping experiences than choosing a book through Puffin's book club mailing program. For those who might have missed it, we'd be handed a colourful pamphlet by our teacher that featured pictures of the latest book offerings from the Puffin company. Each was accompanied by a short blurb and of course a price. We could take these little flyers home, select a book with our parents by ticking the relevant box on the form, and then return it to school in an envelope with the exact change securely within. This would go back to the teacher and then, we assumed, to a large puffin in a suit behind a desk to sort out. Within a few weeks, which surely felt like months, a carton of books would be sent to the classroom and our teacher would read out our names and book titles one by one. It was during these ten minutes or so that our excitement levels would pique closely to Christmas or Easter levels. A brand new book was coming! It was going to be handed to us just like that! How could this be? It was surely magic. And if you were wise, you would have selected something from the only storyteller that mattered at the time, Mr Paul Jennings.

Skating Reflexes

While the death wobbles aren't exactly deadly, they are sufficiently off-putting. At first, your board starts swaying, wavering from its course, then vibrating, eventually tipping and giving way like a punctured raft. Your wheels turn at a seemingly impossible rate, you lose control of the ride and, in the final seconds before impact, you picture yourself catapulting head over heels into black gravel. Ultimately, you catapult from the board, mostly as an instinctive bailout ahead of careening into a parked car ahead. Your elbows and knees, those points that stick out more than, say, a nose—even on an Italian kid—generally take the brunt of the contact. If you're lucky—when you're eleven, your falls tend to be a little more fortuitous—you'll pop up with only bruises and grazes. It'll hurt, but not as much as your ego. That feels like it's been hit by a fire truck.

What you'd give for a hosing down at that point, by the way. Meanwhile, your board, a momentary object of disgust for the crashed skater, scoots from the scene, into the gutter, up a driveway and across some freshly cut lawn. Or it smacks into the rear tyre of an old brown station wagon parked at the end of the street. The board usually escapes unblemished in each scenario.

Though belting into the cement kerb could yield a dent or at least the roughing up of your plastic nose guard—should you have one of those.

In 1986, my brother and I had nondescript wooden skateboards from Kmart, before graduating to brand-name sets of wheels. They were neatly trimmed light wood, yellow wheeled, and partly covered with a layer of black grip tape at each end, which made them easy to steer. The issue with these boards, besides them being noticeably cheap and unimpressive to the local suburban goons—who in hindsight were about as intimidating as the striped shorts their parents made them wear—was they didn't stay true on steep inclines, or over rocky roads. They were entry-level boards really, ideal for the mild incline of most northern Sydney driveways. Ours was a fairly straight stretch and a good place to learn, but neighbouring driveways on our street were pretty damn steep. One of which became a sort of white whale, an unattainable beast and something you could only hope to conquer in your dreams. I'd often imagine attempting such a feat, descending an impossible hill like the one four doors up from us, a windy series of hills posing as a driveway. It was an impossible run and I'd usually chicken out before setting down it, quickly scooching down into either a squat or a little ball in order to stay on top of the board.

This didn't really count, of course, but surviving so that you could enjoy a lamington for afternoon tea was paramount. Of course, you might also need to escape an irate homeowner at the bottom of the driveway, so being able to quickly hop from your board and leap the fence was also top of mind.

We soon moved onto All-Pro boards, sold in the big boys' section of any good department store.

These were slicker because the wood was coated with a glossy white synthetic material and emblazoned with kooky artwork. Somewhere in the art, the less-than-famous 'AP' logo blended in, almost as you would see on a cheap rental surfboard. Mine had an island and palm tree motif in its centre, which I thought was pretty cool until some local rich kids fronted up to the park with their $200 designer boards. These punks couldn't see the irony of their condescension through their Lamda Lamda Lamda fringes. The AP boards were a smooth ride but we inevitably needed to raise the stakes, or skates, as it were.

We soon upgraded to Reflex, a brand of understated neon style, even if not in the eyes of hardcore skaters. We were never hardcore anyway, whatever that is, but enjoyed the sport as much as anything else we did growing up. Skating was a creative pastime that like surfing called for daring and flair. It was also relatively new, having only captured the mass market in the early eighties. And because it required speed, balance and an adventurous mind, skating was sort of anti-establishment in its philosophy. Skaters need hard surfaces, after all, which usually equates to footpaths and driveways—very often your neighbours'. While the local curmudgeons saw skating as a nuisance or public menace, the roll of wheels against the cement ground was like hearing our favourite Aerosmith or Van Halen songs. Well, my Reflex board was as cool as I could imagine: a pale blue painted wood with a check green pattern splashed across half of its base. The wheels were more rounded than I'd seen on previous models and were a striking lime green colour branded with the Reflex logo. The topside was mostly black, on account of its grip tape. It moved noticeably well on any cement or bitumen surface, probably because of its broad axle—or trucks as they're called.

We'd often charge up to the corner shop in the summer heat, like a pack of lions hunting for water, the sort you'd see on those nature shows with British narration and a suspenseful soundtrack. But we sought OJs, possibly one of the greatest icy treats of all time. They were simply bright orange-flavoured oblongs of ice on a stick, with a square bottom and rounded top, as is often the case. The wrapping featured an array of colours from memory, and for some reason, I recall a cartoon character sporting sunnies and throwing an OJ back in TV commercials. But that's standard branding for just about every frozen confectionery, isn't it? Because OJs were around 25 cents each, kids with bigger mouths than their pockets could afford not just a single midday freshener, but several. In fact, our neighbour and pal Jeremy, a native New Zealander and the best skater we knew was known to knock back a number of OJs in one sitting. Not to be outdone, however, his cousin, Grant, who frequently visited from New Zealand, finished twenty OJs in one day! Needless to say, his skate home was relatively sluggish and peppered with terrible moans. Grant was promptly reprimanded by his uncle and soon returned to the Bay of Plenty, plenty bloated.

We used to glide beyond the row of shops and around the end to a bendy path, which would take us behind the supermarket. It was there we'd roll to a pause, absorb our last OJs and then coolly toss the sticks into a large green bin at the rear of the block. We'd then launch down the winding street with excitement because it was the smoothest laid road in the neighbourhood, and aptly called Pleasant Avenue. Skateboarding was one of the best ways to get around, especially if you were a pre-teen with no particular place to go. Chuck Berry's curiosity would have surely run wild had he known the thrill one can achieve on a skateboard.

Soon, a teenage Tony Hawk soared onto the scene, winning the American Skateboarder of the Year award twelve consecutive times, and popping up, and spinning through the air in films, too. When we saw Hawk ripping through inner city streets and flipping over stair rails in one of the *Police Academy* movies, it was truly high art—and motivation. Then there were skateboarding video games adding to the sport's cultural impact, like Skate or Die, where you raced around a park and beat up street hoods or California Games which had the half-pipe and wacky beachside music. They were easy times, more complicated than that of our parents perhaps, but far easier, and slower, than today—at least if pixelated skaters are any benchmark. But by far, the most awe-inspiring skater in my eyes was, you guessed it, Marty McFly. The way he cruised around fictional Hill Valley waving to the aerobics girls and leaping over park benches was, well, cooler than MTV, Dire Straits and *Who's the Boss?* all rolled together. Marty's ultimate trick was latching onto the back of local drivers for a speedy delivery to his destination, courtesy of the usually unaware driver. It was an iconic cinematic moment and confirmation for the Cola War generation that skateboarding was just an incredible concept.

Glammed-Up

The soundtrack of the over-gelled, pink t-shirt, sockless loafer era was equally loud, often featuring the clanging of heavy guitars and drums, synthesised pianos and the operatic screams of wild frontmen. This was the lewd magnetism of glam metal bands like Def Leppard, Poison, Bon Jovi, Motley Crue and Europe. It was pretty intoxicating, their hair as robust as their sound. I recall first seeing Bon Jovi's 'Living On A Prayer' video on Channel 10's *Video Hits* and thinking to myself, could any group of guys be any cooler than this? Or could anyone else get those pants on without pulling a hammy? I mean look at them, are they leather or spandex? Look at their boots, these blokes might be androgynous cowboys. Check out their moves, they're prancing around and leaping off things like jungle monkeys. And the way they sing … on occasion, they'd crowd around the main microphone and belt it out together, as close to a smooch as you might get in a public setting. Is the money tighter than it seems for these guys that they can't each have a mic? Above all, was the music, though. For the eighties youth, their lyrics were inspiring and the way in which lead man Jon Bon Jovi screamed them out, demanded that you come along with him, that you take notice, even if people made fun of your striped tights and tasselled boots. These guys could do anything—they were the musical equivalent of Michael Jordan, boasting skill, determination, attitude and a flair for the impossible. How could anyone not sing along, 'We'll Give it a Shot!'

There was certainly something about the anthems of Bon Jovi and Motley Crue that were indicative of the eighties cultural sentiment—it was defiance and a touch of decadence. Not that such a thing resonated with my ten-year-old self but in retrospect, it was a kind of rebellion without there really being anything to rebel against, not like during prior decades of the sixties or seventies, ravaged by political corruption and terrible wars. The eighties had some of that, sure, but was a better time in one sense because nothing seemed to bother our parents too much in quiet suburbia. Perhaps it was less intensely reported, which is distinctively unlike the 2020s, where the media tells us we're in a new version of Armageddon every other month. Maybe there just aren't enough wild frontmen anymore, snarling in the face of the establishment. Maybe we need their attitude, their outlandish hair and nonsensical lyrics, the leaping around the stage and self-indulgent guitar solos—a little kick in the leather chaps with a snakeskin boot.

I also want to beat the drum—er, I mean—electronic drums a bit. Paired with a similarly plugged-in piano and a couple of guitars, and you had something synthetically magical. There were many bands that adopted this strategy, including Duran Duran, Depeche Mode, Eurythmics and The Pet Shop Boys. But there was one group that managed to electrify everything while simultaneously sounding like a traditional rock n' roll band, and given that they hailed from Sydney, there was reason for us to love them even more. The metallic rattle and romp of INXS's album 'Kick' charged into

1987 with enough gigawatts to send us kids to the future and back.

Not even the nuclear-powered DeLorean could have kept pace in this instance. The first time I heard the album sitting in the front room of my house, the chords tore through my Sony Walkman and bolted across the space, before boomeranging back to slap me across the cheek. Hey, I deserved it. I believe Kick overrode the senses of every teenager it struck. But I was just eleven, so I thought lead man Michael Hutchence was referring to an evenly contested soccer match when he bellowed, something about hoofing it. Certainly, I was too young to appreciate the emotion of INXS's most iconic record and yet, there I was, lying on the floor of our family home, just a short drive from where the boys went to high school in northern Sydney, absorbing the record's boom and bravado.

In truth, I came to the tape by accident because Andy, surely drawn to the crisp cut-outs of people depicted on the cover, which included a band member on a skateboard, bought it for me as a gift. That's as good a reason to buy an album as any with only a decade of life experience under your belt. I guess I'm forever indebted to Andy for making that choice. I remain less enthused about 'Girl You Know It's True' by Milli Vanilli, but that's for another day. INXS's impact all boggles the mind decades later, after the record sold 14 million copies, 8 million in the US alone. Arsenio, Rosie, shiny accolades and copious amounts of drugs followed. It was a wild piece of pop culture work in hindsight. It really took my untainted ears a few listens to get into it. But it was all so hypnotic, repetitive even, as it slid over to us with moves so raw. It didn't seem possible that someone could write lyrics like this! And so as Kick re-entered the local lexicon and rocketed up the Australian pop charts once again in 2014, I couldn't help, but smile. I imagined that somewhere in Sydney, an unsuspecting 11-year-old was playing the album on his iPod for the first time, and was equally overjoyed.

So much did the synthesiser fill our little ear drums that every pre-teen wanted one of their own. My sister had one, a bulky Casio number with sound effects, drum beats and in-built tunes.

There were pleasing rubber buttons to press and flickering lights to enjoy, which we all did in between her piano lessons. We might have donned a headband or some dark shades too, maybe a cool t-shirt with a skull and crossbones—it was time to rock…or pop, as it were. There was so much to draw on for inspiration. There was Donna Summer's 'I Feel Love,' for example, which boasted quintessential keyboard sounds, fast and rhythmic. It was science fiction turned melodic. Then in David Bowie's 'Under Pressure' the synth was more complimentary and yet still so integral. Who can forget Van Halen's 'Jump?' The electronic piano was really the core of the production, the signature notes for a guitar-centric band. If you think about it, the eighties keyboardist was pretty fringe, too. I mean it wasn't like Jon Bon Jovi made his bread and butter tickling the ivories, nor did Van Halen want their guitar hero, Eddie, to be seen on stage behind a Roland. No, the keyboards were typically set up in the back or off to the side where one lonesome soul would tap away at a supplementary riff. This sidekick status, if you like, is perhaps what makes us all the more nostalgic for the humble synth.

Even years later, the keyboard is capable of making any song better, and many of today's music stars appear intent on following that premise. Take R&B artist *The Weekend*, whose track 'Blinding Lights' is something you would have heard blasting out of a convertible Trans Am in 1984. Meanwhile, his song 'In Your Eyes' might have accompanied a couple snuggling in the car parked up at the lookout. It's a weird time travel we're currently doing in pop music, but it's also a welcome and familiar sound for those of a certain age.

Sandshoe Champs

Sports Day was the best back in '83, remember? Once a week you'd be lucky enough to go to school in a t-shirt and sandshoes, barely able to contain your joy that half the day would be devoted to kicking, hitting or throwing a ball. What a country! This grand tradition continues in 2024, of course, and so this section is as much a celebration of an enduring school-time routine as it is a recollection. It's equally a nod to the simplicity of sports days past, often on very scrubby pitches, pot-holed playgrounds and with well-worn equipment—none of which inhibited the grand experience of it all. Do you remember your school sports house? I was in the 'Wattle' house in primary school, named for the flower. Yes, we were yellow, though I wouldn't concede that was indicative of our temperament. Our rivals were 'Waratah' (red), 'Jacaranda' (blue) and 'Boronia' (green). Now, let's get real here: Wattle was the best team. We weren't the fastest, sure. And we didn't scoop up all the trophies. Fine, but we were the best because when we closed our eyes and hoped for a victory we simply felt it, like Obi-Wan working over some poor sap with The Force.

A lot of sport at the school level is built around Star Wars-level ambition if little else. It was all about bragging rights. Your house was better than that of your best friend. Your buddy's house, it was argued back, won more. Sometimes you even ended up on the same losing side.

Confused? Such was the complex relationship eight-year-olds had with their house. Well, it all came to a head on sports day, when high-stakes games like tunnel ball, captain ball, kickball and the wonderfully Aussie version of handball (or 'hando') separated the men and women from the boys and girls. It was truly glorious to turn up to school on a Friday in your favourite sneakers, anticipating, the gladiatorial feats that lay ahead (as long as your mum didn't buy you a random no-frills brand called 'Apple Pie,' as mine did). How on earth we digested our lunchtime meat pies and sausage rolls on such days remains a mystery, one that I'm sure George Negus is still researching for a mothballed 60 Minutes segment. Nonetheless, the sport was fierce, spirited and so much fun that it made the school week completely worthwhile. My game of choice was kickball. It allowed those of us who dreamed of booting a ball like Liverpool's Craig Johnston to unleash hell on an unsuspecting Spalding volleyball. Watching that helpless dusty sphere set sail across the blue summer sky and over the fence was a thing of beauty. You'd then scurry around the bases like a pinstriped New York Yankee, whom you could only really imagine having never seen such a thing beyond the movies.

Other sports days were more Aussie in tone, of course, like the many times we played Kanga Cricket. It was essentially cricket but as I recall with a softer yellow ball and a goofy plastic bat. I liked it because the real red leather careening down the pitch towards your Jatz Crackers was more than unnerving. Armed with only the box in the sports master's bag for protection, one wondered how our sadistic PE teachers remained employed.

How many people wore that thing, anyway? Yes, Kanga was more my pace and also let the soccer players among us get our eye in among the mini Waughs and Boons who'd spawned during the mid-eighties.

Otherwise, we might be lucky enough to play touch footy again and perhaps rehash our weekend party movies. Footy also started conversations, as I've alluded to. Friends would ask me who my favourite team was and I'd say, "Parra, who else?" In '83 that was the password for access into any social circle (I believe Indiana Jones also used it to open the Ark of the Covenant!). If, however, you were mates with the other mob across the playground, then you said, "Manly—the mighty Sea Eagles." It's amazing that we all got along so well. For mine, this is where our fascination with sport begins. I'm assuming you share this view and most probably relate to my primary school experience in the suburbs of northern Sydney. These formative years—on the playground with mates, tossing and kicking a ball, then watching Sunday footy on the telly with Mum and Dad, and venturing to the local park to see your team play—it all tends to stir something up. I suppose it's a tribal connection, something we can feel a part of. But sport is also uncomplicated—unlike real life. This makes it endlessly appealing and I think we realise that very early on.

What You Talkin' 'Bout, Willis?

There was something very distinct about TV we watched as kids, especially the sitcoms that separate the 1980s from almost all other eras. The most recognisable format of the day was the 'family sitcom' and not the sitcoms of the sixties that were really more about escapism, such as *Gilligan's Island*, *Bewitched* or *I Dream of Jeanie*. TV content in our time was trying to expand and, so for a moment, felt closer to the seventies tone of real-life relationships and issues. I'd suggest that American shows like *Maude*, *The Brady Bunch*, *Good Times, Happy Day*s and British comedies like *Steptoe and Son*, and *Porridge* offered a bridge to a new era. But while the seventies programmes were noticeably grittier than the idealised sixties shows, the eighties sitcom was still different again, shinier perhaps, faster paced and typically concluded with an upbeat tone.

In my mind the family structures and plots tried to reflect reality but were certainly pushing the definition of 'everyday life'—think *Alf, Perfect Strangers, Who's The Boss, Diff'rent Strokes* and *The Facts Of Life.* The eighties version of the sitcom was therefore a sort of hybrid, somewhat familiar familial relationships, wholesome suburban settings, some wacky plots and the occasional semi-serious incident—but a warm cuddle to finish up. I think this provided a perfect balance because after school while munching on some chicken Twisties and downing a tall glass of Cottee's lemon cordial, I couldn't think of anything better than tuning into the daggy dreamer, Tony Micelli, or the warm family antics on *Growing Pains* giving us saccharine morality. Sure they were corny. Yes, many of the jokes came with a wink and smile. And of course, the stereotypes were a bit forced by today's standards. Big deal, tastes were different folks, so much so that we supported any suburban family unit with a 23-minute tale to tell each week. There was a full-head-of-hair dad calling out all the moral shortcomings of others; the peppy and typically blonde mum always keeping the family afloat; and the kids who were cheeky but mostly well-intentioned. They were caricatures and we tuned in because they made us feel good.

A lot of shows were on all the time, the repetition of syndication almost part of the package, lulling you into loving even the most aimless programme. These shows also had uppity theme songs, overly produced canned laughter, and plenty of yuks in between sentimental moments. I mean it wasn't the Golden Age of TV as people like to claim of television nowadays, but it was creative, heartfelt and the shows were popular because at their core was some genuinely funny writing. Yes, the creators took a lighter touch, preferring to explain any problem away in the time it took to finish a McCain TV dinner. This allowed its audience to tune in 'next time' with a clean slate. In other words, we didn't really come for the heavy stuff. We signed on for the good-looking kids and their cool attitudes, as well as their jokey parents like Jason and Maggie Seaver and the Huxtables. This was frivolous TV, I suppose, but there was a sense of casualness that I liked about it. What can I say? We didn't have drug dealers and dragons. We had light-hearted jibes, puffed-up hair and screen-wide grins. It was delicious cotton candy for those with a sweet tooth.

It goes without saying that we had sweet little things at breakfast too, among them Coco the Monkey, Sam Toucan and Honey Bear. Such TV mascots appeared onscreen often when we were growing up, perhaps in short bursts only but always with long impact. Any given ad break during Space Ghost or Romper Room might see one of them pop up to tell us about the virtues of Coco Pops, Fruit Loops and Honey Smacks. They had kooky voices and quirky catchphrases that we'd run around the house echoing, "Just like a chocolate milkshake, only cruuuuuuunchy," being one of our favourites. There were other characters too, including Tony the Tiger who cheerfully growled about Frosties, "Theeeey're grrr-eat!" Tony also doled out free rollerblading advice to those kids short of balance. Then there was Snap, Crackle and Pop, those fun elfish blokes in hats, always intent on making rice bubbles fun. And they were—how could they not be with jovial sprites like that springing around the screen?

While all these cereals are still available today, you don't see the mascots as much and that's a shame. Yes, they're on the packaging but their voices certainly aren't as pervasive as they were in ninety-eighty-something. I mean "Get your own Honey Smacks! Get your own Honey Smacks!" was as commonly heard down our front hallway as "Mum, have you seen my swimmers?" But times change and even Sam Toucan can't endear himself to everyone!

Still, I have nothing but fond memories of mornings with those characters selling us intensely sweet kick-starters, the type of classic cereal nibbles that brilliantly complemented our early hours with Hong Kong Phooey, The Flintstones and

Spiderman. I mean how might any six-year-old in the history of time absorb such wacky concepts as a karate-chopping canine, a stone-age family in suburbia or a web-slinging teenager without coloured sugar loops or puffs of cocoa? It wasn't possible, which is why the cereal people so cleverly gave us friendly TV mascots to bridge the gap. Genius.

Late Night Moods

TV chatter took on other forms, too. The talk show as we know it started way back in TV history, and nerds of the box might even cite famous American late night hosts like Steve Allen, Dick Cavett and Jack Paar. Some might mention Michael Parkinson in Britain or Graham Kennedy and Bert Newton in Australia. These men were undoubtedly the pioneers of the format, but once again it was a more modern generation that took things a step further. Indeed, for many, the 1980s saw the apex of talk shows.

This seems a fair call to me because as the great Johnny Carson took his longstanding act into the eighties, we were additionally spoiled by a fresh batch of new hosts, some of whom had the gift of the gab, others the gift of the gag! It was this combination of talents that really makes the period stands out for its high-end late-night TV offerings, the sorts of shows that you tuned in to as a matter of routine. I mean eighties TV host names read like a who's who of the broadcasting hall of fame, from Sally Jesse Raphael and Oprah Winfrey, to Phil Donahue and David Letterman. There was Arsenio Hall, Regis Philbin, Geraldo Rivera, Ricki Lake and Merv Griffin, too. How about Joan Rivers? Or Ray Martin here in Oz? I mean seriously—the talking talent on TV was immense back then and at a time when the format was really revered. They didn't just give any old Joe Schmoe a show, folks, this was the big time at the biggest time. To put this in better context, we only need to consider Oprah's 25-year run to see that the eighties was a springboard for many of the greatest TV talking heads. Such was Oprah's impact and reach that her show was beamed to 145 countries, and according to her own website, she received more than 20 million letters over that two and half decade span. I don't even think Justin Bieber could boast those numbers.

There's something even more significant that I want to raise about retro-era talk shows and that's the mood they set. There were two strands to this: self-help conversation and the self-deprecating host. Neither was new in the eighties but each factor quickly became a trope, honed by the masters of this TV genre like no one else before. Take Letterman, who made self-deprecating jokes an art form on his *Late Show* programme, where yes, he was happy to poke fun at guests but was just as adept and degrading himself for a laugh. It's what made Dave the king of late-night television for a long time. A classic Dave segue might have simply been, "What else are we doing tonight? Right…other stuff? All kinds of fun stuff tonight ladies and gentlemen." Similarly, few handled the problems of everyday Americans like Donahue and Oprah. They set the standard for being good listeners while holding a microphone among 300 complete strangers. There's no denying that their work in front of studio audiences became the template for what followed in daytime talk thereafter. The sort of in-public confession and subsequent therapy that took place on such shows was actually once called 'Oprahfication' by *The Wall Street Journal*. Indeed, Oprah and her contemporaries took the good ol' powwow to new levels. So, combining the skills and savvy of these gifted performers is not only something to recollect and fire up again on YouTube but perhaps deserves a spot in the annals of pop culture iconography. They set the cultural mood. Think about it: during the day, we might have lamented our inability to show empathy or forgiveness and so sought some quick self-help, while at night we could laugh it all off because Dave just tossed a football at a meatball atop a Christmas tree. The eighties truly introduced us to the full spectrum of TV moods and in a very real sense, they resonated well beyond their hour-long slots.

The mood wasn't lost on us kids either, because during the holidays we'd indulge in plenty of meaningless daytime TV, much of it spearheaded by Phil and Oprah. I remember one day amid Nintendo rounds and backyard cricket, we got out of the sun to take in some Donahue, you know, for kicks. Our buddy John popped in and for some reason brought a microphone with him. He was a real movie buff and so always had cameras and funny equipment lying around his house. So, he hooked up the mic to our VCR and started recording his voice over a segment of the Donahue Show he had taped earlier. He picked up Phil's stop-start style brilliantly, mimicking his accent and tone, almost perfectly in sync with the host's moving mouth. Andy and I were in stitches, rolling around the floor as John also dubbed funny voices over members of the audience sharing their stories with Phil. But instead of using the actual dialogue, John said things like, "Phil, I'm worried because my three kids eat too much butter! They're gaining a lot of weight, Phil, and it's because of the butter, I'm sure of it," he said into the mic as a stressed out mum in the audience.

Then, without missing a beat, he'd dub Phil's herky-jerky response, "So… your… kid… is eating too much butter! And we'll be back in just a moment." Growing up in front of the TV wasn't all bad.

The Chase Scene

It's probably best that we're realistic about the overall attitude of the culture in say, 1987: it was big, loud, confident and buoyed by a workforce that wanted excess and success. That's when the movie *Wall Street came* out and it surely exemplified some of this desire—the obsessive focus on money, overly indulgent luxury, superfluous glamour, hard drugs and being a prolific consumer...to you know, consume stuff. 'Greed is good!' the film's villain Gordon Gekko cried. I can't deny that this all went on, but I was a kid so my recollection is blurry and only tinged by the positive glow of the adults around me, and indeed blocked by the largeness of some people's embellished eighties-era hair. But for the most part, it was a fun experience for the pre-teen.

For those of us fortunate enough to grow up in a comfortable family life and good neighbourhoods, there was an assortment of amusements on offer. You might even say that the trickle-down of mass consumption brought about carnival-level delight: consider Masters Of The Universe figurines, Hubba Bubba bubble-gum, *Jaws and Rocky* VHS tapes, Harlem Globetrotter basketballs, fluorescent blue and green water pistols, Jawbreaker candy balls, Pound Puppies, Wonder Boy, Bubble O'Bills, Slush Puppies, bright red novelty sunglasses, acid wash jeans, Air Jordans, plastic robot claws, Reebok Pump sneakers, headbands, Tetris, *Purple Rain,* and the purple Care Bear with the rainbow belly. It was all such good stuff, honestly. So, it'd be rather tricky and perhaps disingenuous for someone like me—wearing rose-tinted nostalgia goggles—to offer a grumpy BBC-historian style retrospective lamenting the bravado of the times. So, let's take a different approach.

Perhaps the place that best exemplifies the eighties ethos is the shopping mall, typically a building filled with every retailer in town and beyond. What the mall represents is the ability to shop non-stop, all day and for just about anything your heart desires. Anything you might think up, really, be it tennis sneakers, car cleaner, watches, freshly squeezed juice, skateboards, power tools, sandwiches, Christmas ornaments, imported linens, ping pong tables, framed posters, novelty toys, freshly baked cookies, designer dresses or lounge suits—they were pretty much all available within the few floors of the mall. And this remains the case today, of course, which tells us what a brilliant concept the original shopping blocks were. This little retail plan took off so much that the geniuses at Mall HQ decided to go one further. Thus the mall was expanded to become the 'mega-mall,' a giant consumer-centric space that not only appealed to the spender but the diner, the casual loiterer and those who liked to sip takeaway coffee while sitting by an indoor fountain. These were indeed mega-spaces, usually built over more than 800,000 square feet, where the building's designers could conjure up indoor luxuriating around elaborate pools of water, bright flower beds, piazzas and sculptures. The princely boulevards and vistas within were perfect representations of the time: shiny, expensive, broad and audacious. They were areas for consumers to overwork their credit cards and for mall rats to overestimate their skateboarding skills. The mega-mall was sanitised and safe, as long as you liked to buy lots of stuff, scoff down food court noodles and breathe in recycled air. And who among us doesn't excel at such tasks?

Growing up I spent a lot of time in Chatswood Chase, an eighties-era mega-mall for the eager-to-spend folks of Sydney's middle north shore. The Chase, which is still around, has always been a bit fancy and so I can't say that it offered us kids a lot—though it has always boasted plenty of space! And it was actually the space we sought. Many a Saturday Andy, John, and I would stop by the Norgen Vaaz ice cream shop on the sprawling ground floor for a round of vanilla milkshakes, before heading upstairs to the Luxury Level to lounge about. Up a few escalators and we found ourselves almost alone, where we kicked back and watched the world go by below, acting like little kings on the soft couches that centre management had dotted around this exclusive carpeted floor. There were only a few stores up that high in this enormous building, most of which seemed rather quiet, possibly because they were too far away, or maybe because they were a little bit random. Some malls still work this way, forgetting the top level almost entirely. The ongoing commitment to weird floor plans aside, it's much harder to find a really good milkshake in today's mega-mall!

Under the Pillow Status

For an alarming number of people, it's impossible to believe that the footy club, the Parramatta Eels, were once more popular than the South Sydney Rabbitohs. This stings as an Eels fan and as someone, who is often met with either a smirk or sympathetic frown when I refill my Eels-branded coffee mug in the office kitchen, it's like Tiger Balm down the shorts. Of course, if we consider the lowly existence of Souths over the forty years after 1970, just about any rugby league club could be regarded as popular by comparison. (Okay, in the decades prior to this Souths was a mighty outfit, perhaps the mightiest of all. And so, I tip my hat to the many older fans out there). Anyway, when measuring clubs, I'm talking about more than mere ticket sales, membership tallies or the number of celebrities photographed with a supporter cap on. I'm referring to cultural significance.

The Eels were once a sporting institution and a force to be reckoned with in the eighties, at a time when there was fierce competition for pop culture currency from the likes of The A-Team and Sonic The Hedgehog. Still, even as I write this, I realise the idea is inconceivable to millennials or Gen Zers, especially given that Parra is now one of the most enigmatic footy clubs you'll come across. I mean if the Eels are ever seen to be dismantling your favourite team on a Saturday afternoon, rest assured that they'll eventually turn on themselves, affording your mob a genuine chance at a comeback. This has been commonplace for a club that once destroyed all opponents before half-time. Okay, slight exaggeration. They at least made irreversible damage by the time Ray Price went into his exhausted hands-on-hips pose. Without a doubt, orange halves would have been the highlight of the afternoon for many teams when they faced the Eels. Between 1981 and 1985 it was an absolute truth that the Eels weren't just great, they were iconic.

The only way I think I might prove this to you is to explain the value of the ultimate football currency: trading cards. In the era of high socks and headbands, the trading card of a high-profile Eels star, say, Peter Sterling, Brett Kenny or Eric Grothe, could reduce an eight-year-old to a pair of bulging eyeballs, the kind that sprung from Roger Rabbit's head. And that was just the cards.

The Scanlens stickers and sticker book were on another level. The pics on the stickers were always classic action shots like the Eels' Stan Jurd looking as though he might be relieving himself while clutching the ball in 1984. Similarly, the scrunched face of Norths' Don McKinnon before copping a clothesline in 1983 is a thing of beauty. What was it about these little photos printed on cardboard? I suppose it was that they were both mementoes of a sport we enjoyed watching each winter weekend, but also something we could collect and treasure as if they were our own photos. We'd bundle loads of them, tightly bounding the collection with a pink rubber band from a top drawer somewhere in the house. The sides of the few cards on top of that pile might bend a little, but that didn't matter. You could always put 'doubles' on top, or perhaps a few cards you weren't that fond of—for me that'd be someone from the Rabbits forward pack or a random winger from the Penrith Panthers. Either way, your cards were appreciated like a wallet, often accompanying you to school in case a game of card flicks broke out. The aim was to toss a card you were willing to part with as far as possible, hoping to reach a mark that was too good for your opponent, who subsequently launched a card in the same direction. The winner would be rewarded with both cards.

Alternatively, you might see who could toss the card and position it closest to a wall or bench in the playground, a much tougher assignment requiring a deft touch. I was never willing to risk an Eel such as Sterling or Kenny for this type of thing; so if another Parramatta fan fronted up for a challenge, I'd either try bargain for a straight-up trade, or I'd offer a flick game featuring lesser players. Every team had a supporting cast, of course, those players that typically posted good statistics but perhaps didn't win your heart. So, it was easy enough to part with a card boasting a lot of tries or tackles made if that player wasn't one of your favourites. Confronted with a proposal to flick Sterling or his doppelganger, fullback Paul Taylor, I was forced to go with Taylor every time (sorry, Paul!)

Scanlens was originally a trading cards company in the 1930s and sold cards featuring everything from Disney characters to *Planet of the Apes*. And like all good card makers over the years, they shoved a stick of chewing gum in every pack. That sweet fleeting flavour never leaves you. The first sports-themed cards were produced in limited quantities in the early sixties, usually focused on Aussie rules and cricket. By the seventies and eighties rugby league and even soccer cards had ramped up. Indeed, many of the collections between 1963 and 1989 are said to be real collectors' items. I can at least vouch for the league sticker books from those truly rad years.

One year, I think it was '83, they even had glossy logo stickers for each team, usually set on a silver or gold background. They seemed especially hard to come by and that made trading for them a high-stress affair on the playground. There was just a little extra weight to those stickers, which ultimately added some bulk to one's sticker book—the truest measure of a good collector. But the pièce de résistance was the back cover of the '83 league album which had cartoon logos for all of 14 New South Wales teams. Those caricatures added so much to my enjoyment of the competition because, for the first time, I could visualise the clubs as anthropomorphic animals. I can't explain it really, but those crazy-eyed cartoon logos tearing through their respective team emblems were so joyful that they elevated the Scanlens book to, well, Under-the-Pillow status. Even my prized Han Solo figure had to make room.

Jolly on the Spot

Perhaps the connective fibre of the Pac-Man Generation was mass marketing—a bolder and brighter promotion of the good life, attained by frantically gobbling power pellets within a neon maze, or otherwise. But what was *good*? And how did one acquire it? One word: branding! Most popular brands back then boasted outsized fun and an acute sense of excitement, but maybe that was just the way my family felt. We loved the TV commercials at the time because they seemed to invite us in and ask us to crack open a cold soft drink or dive into some cheesy chips along with the people in the ad. There was an open invitation in such commercials. I think maybe there was ambiguity too, because ads from our favourite drink makers and sneaker brands often came with a play on words and a wink. I guess you were in, or you weren't. I suppose a person loved the upbeat Glen Fry number or was desperately searching for the clicker.

Given that most of the ads in my memory were mass brand spots on a national, and maybe even international scale, I imagined the majority of people were on board. The stuff on offer was often very cool by virtue of the fact that it had been repackaged in a slick 30-second commercial that relied on fewer words and more on the way it made us feel. One Pepsi ad that stands out in my memory is a summer beach scene, tanned bodies laying out in the heat, the surf splashing…and a prankster teenager in a nearby van popping a bottle of Pepsi, pouring it over ice in a glass and then gulping down—all in front of a live mic that blasts the enticing sounds out to hundreds of thirsty beachgoers. He then opens the back of the van full of Pepsi to meet the salivating customers surrounding him. This was so very appealing, mostly because there was no blatant coercion. In this style of ad, which is typical of the era, the push is replaced by a sense of cheekiness that, as I say, lures you in to be part of a very cool product. The eighties ad people also mastered the celebrity-driven commercial and Michael J Fox's appearances for the soft drink exemplified how associating with the hottest people of the moment could also turn any brand into a hot commodity. The ad where Fox darts out of his apartment and into a rainy night to hunt down a Pepsi for his thirsty and attractive neighbour is among the best. The brand gets instant cache with Fox, but in addition, the mini-movies they essentially created for him help position the product as a must-have item for anyone with the desire to be youthful and sexy…so just about everyone.

There was something else about all these advertisements that may shock the uninitiated—they were downright likeable! It's hard to pinpoint why exactly, and there's also the possibility that I adored Fox and that he and other big names of the eighties still make me happy. While this is surely true in part, I suspect there's more to it, that if today's ad people at least applied the same sense of fun to their TV spots instead of always seemingly trying to outsmart the audience, they might actually resonate with us. While I'm not certain that Tom Holland or Andrew Garfield playing the cool guy in the Manhattan apartment would work, I do think I'd enjoy it a lot more than the over-amplified, trying-to-be-too-clever and ultra-obscure commercials of some of today's brands. In fact, I'm sure I'd gravitate more towards the mini-movie idea than say, the middle-aged guy in the SUV spewing nonsense to his family as some clichéd rock anthem cranks up. No, a celebrity scurrying down a fire escape in the pouring rain to round up some Pepsi is way more fun than the preachy four-wheel-driving hipster dad taking his car over ludicrously rough terrain. Look, if you don't have a good idea, or Michael J Fox for that matter, I think you may as well scrap the script and simply flash the product and price on the screen. Short of a movie-style idea, there was a spoonful of sugar. What I mean is, syrupy language and smiles, and certain celebrities can deliver better than others.

Athletes are particularly good at this delivery, such as eighties bad boy tennis star, Andre Agassi. 'Image is everything,' claimed a wild-haired Agassi in a 1980s ad-spot for Canon, as he removed his dark sunglasses and looked down the lens, the glass apparently dripping with golden syrup. The ad was glossy and so clichéd in its message you'd think Donald Trump wrote it in a tweet. There was something very memorable about sports ads in the eighties and in Australia, our active lifestyle helped with the push. Many of our favourite sporting mega-stars were beamed to us directly, product in hand, syrup running off their cue cards. The likes of Michael Jordan, Greg Norman, Chris Evert, Jimmy Connors, Mary Lou Retton and Pat Cash were everywhere, as were the drinks, chips, hamburgers or insurance brands they typically spruiked. As such, advertising morphed and manifested another vibe, one that was kind of cool because it featured people whose physical prowess demanded our adoration and attention. I mean if anyone was suitable enough to tell us about deodorant it was Charles Barkley.

Personally, I love a syrupy product push from an athlete I'm fond of. The idea that someone so dominant in their respective field can be convinced to promote an item they may never have seen before, and then deliver the message with wooden conviction, is both intriguing and remarkable. But even more than that, I always enjoyed the staged reality of athlete-led advertising, whether it was a locker room scene, or after an everyday workout telling us how they stay refreshed, the way an oh-so-calm Jimmy Connors did with Lipton Ice Tea in the early nineties. There was something rather quirky and inspiring about it all, especially those larger-than-life pitches from America.

Despite the significant distance from Hollywood, especially at a time when big overseas trips were far less frequent, we felt connected to those stars because the ads gave a unique insight into their life. I suppose this was the point. The ad people were opening the door to the lives of superstars in a way that hadn't been seen before. They were able to convince us that bitter on-field football rivals might actually meet in the shadowy tunnel of a quietened stadium after the Super Bowl and joke over Diet Pepsi. Hey, it could happen. And we all had our favourites. I was immediately drawn to any ads by Converse or Nike, and more often than not the spots with famous American basketballers. One such ad featured legends Magic Johnson and Larry Bird facing off in a game of one-on-one hoops in the Middle of Nowhere, Indiana, each sporting their specially designed Converse sneakers. 'The Magic shoe, the Bird shoe,' the deep and raspy narrator started, "Choose your weapon!" This was a sublime copy to my twelve-year-old mind, an ad with real-life impact. An ad that represented the world I wanted to be in, even more so because it wasn't part of our local media landscape, but something that might only be discovered during a weekend sports show like *Wide World Of Sports* or deep within a pirated copy of *Top Gun* on video tape.

Big Hype Fashion

No conversation about our retro lives would be complete without delving into the era's much-loved fashion trends. Who knew the styles of our youth would hold up? They really seemed of a time—bright, striped, white, hyper, denim, skinny, big-shouldered, boofy and baggy. It's really hard to describe what was going on but what we can say is that many of the eighties' most adored fashion trends live on today. It's a weird thing the cycle of fashion, especially when it looked for all money that the eighties tableau would not be repeated.

And yet here we are in 2024, with teenagers wearing white sneakers like eighties jocks, denim jackets being paired with denim jeans like in my favourite old sitcoms, and of course, classic black sunnies slid on with Tom Cruise determination. Everyone seems to want a piece of the eighties style in their current ensemble, from 16-year-olds to 50-somethings. I kind of get the nostalgic oldies, but to see a 21-year-old go denim on denim over a neon pink t-shirt and laced up in a pair of Jordan sneakers seems surprising. Similarly, black Ray Ban sunglasses worn by the likes of the *Blues Brothers* in 1980 have become a staple yet again. Some cultural critics such as Chuck Klosterman say the reason for all this is in part due to the internet and its ubiquity, whereby cultural artefacts of the recent past have been made so readily available to new generations that they can quite literally scoop and sample bits and pieces from an endlessly wide ocean. In other words, so much of what defined the life and times of previous decades has been usurped by a very static period in which *all* pop culture is available for recycling. Hence, a poster of my guy Fox sporting denim and white sneakers in '85 feels very contemporary.

Similarly, the teenagers in the *Breakfast Club* wearing an array of eighties classics from Judd Nelson's jacket to Molly Rongwald's pink t-shirt and Ally Sheedy's high-top sneakers, all seem pretty on point for a day in high school in 2023. Or take a leopard print anything, brightly coloured Lycra tights, overalls and jackets with shoulder pads—it's hard to imagine any of these items getting called out on a Reddit fashion advice channel. They'd surely be lauded by the internet fashionistas of today. How about a brilliant yellow raincoat, a polka dot dress, a very wide belt or a baggy sweater with randomly placed bright coloured triangles printed all over it? It's all going to work in the 2020s.

But what was the most iconic of eighties fashions? Tough one, but it's got to be when tops went from the seventies' ugly wide lapels and painted-on tightness to bagginess and branded bravado. Eighties t-shirts had attitude and colour. They were unapologetic and bold. Many had large lettering or logos, while others had abstract prints with geometric shapes, dots and lines. I used to love the brightly coloured surfer t-shirts Mum would buy us, many of them boasting chequered patterns and fluorescent stripes, or weirdly shaped animals like the Mambo dog, or a crocodile wearing shades. There were swirls of bright blue representing waves and splattering of eye-popping pink that suggested…well, I'm not so sure but it was cool nonetheless. There were palm trees and setting suns, cartoon surfer dudes and silhouetted windsurfers.

Sometimes there was a flourish of zigs, or zags, or a whir of dots, perhaps even the outlines of a long-haired rider mastering a monster wave, whatever the design, kids in the eighties like them bright and baggy.

Similarly, big print fleecy jumpers that were once the domain of eighties rap artists like the Beastie Boys or Run DMC are now worn anew, even though we hardly have enough cold weather to warrant them! I'm not going to lie, while it might be too warm for fleece hoodies most of the year here, it does warm my heart to see these styles again. I just wish I could wear them without looking like a desperately nostalgic dad. That's the weird thing about fashion—it can come back but also truly pass you by. For instance, I have an old photo of me as a kid sitting in my living room sporting some pretty slick Reebok tennis shoes, the kind that a lot of people are wearing today. I feel oddly proud of this fashion choice and yet thirty years later it might be a stretch for me to pull on the same style of sneakers. Not saying I couldn't, but I'm certain some cool dudes from the local high school would be snickering behind my back in line at KFC.

Ugh, I shouldn't eat any more nuggets, anyway.

Off to the Races

Big events were amped up when we were kids, many of which were made for TV. There was the 1984 Olympics for a start, which was the first time I remember even watching such a thing. I recall filling out my pocket-sized Olympics logbook from the newsagent, in which you could pen the winners, record breakers and scores. 'Carl Lewis' is a name I remember writing, not really sure how anyone could be as quick as he was, covering 100 metres of red rubber track in just a smidge under ten seconds. Lewis was fast and flamboyant and probably talked too much, but with his perfect hair and high-pitched voice, he seemed the perfect complement to a bold era of glamourised pop culture. I mean can you imagine throwing on Michael Jackson's 'Beat It' while watching Lewis race beyond space and time? Such a move might have sent our home appliances into self-combustion and the dog running for the hills.

Thankfully, there were other distractions we could turn to, so as to alleviate potential implosions caused by too much excitement. For example, horse racing was popular and generally deemed less offensive at the time, at least in part because the adults around us appreciated the history of great races like the Melbourne Cup. Unlike today's widely held view that the Cup shouldn't be praised and that it's cruel to the horses, Aussies back then were less likely to ask questions about a thing so steeped in tradition. Personally, I think there's great validity in tradition, which isn't to say everything should stay the same. But there is such a thing as a happy middle ground.

When I first saw a real horse, it was on television in first grade, as my teacher rolled out a wooden TV set atop a trolley for us to watch 'The Cup.' Given my dad was really into the races, this seemed completely normal to my six-year-old mind, though I suspect was pretty odd to most of my little mates in that class. Some probably figured an episode of Quick Draw McGraw was coming on. Being November and the low-tech times of 1982, the classroom was obscenely hot with the only relief from a pedestal fan that always looked to be on its last rotation.

Nevertheless, a chestnut gelding by the name of Kiwi won that cup and we cheered in a frenzied stupor. I still don't know why we were so moved by a New Zealand horse winning a race in a city most of us had never heard of, but this was perhaps our primer for years of sporting obsession to come. The manner in which Kiwi stormed down the home straight like a brown Porsche, clearly piqued our attention. We didn't realise he was a 10-1 outsider, of course, but whispers from the adults in the room that this was a surprising result, surely appealed to us as small kids with an instinctive feel for underdogs. It was a concept that had been fuelled by the impossible efforts of Luke Skywalker, Captain Caveman and Skippy the Bush Kangaroo. Now we were ready for the real thing!

The focus on grand sporting events had indeed been building that same year. Only two months earlier we witnessed an equally impressive moment when an Australian yacht called 'Australia II' wrestled the America's Cup from a mob of American sailors who'd never previously lost it.

The US boat, more poetically named 'Liberty', won the first and second races of that '82 event by margins of more than a minute. Think about when you're waiting for a late train and how long one minute can feel. You could polish off a bag of Smiths' chips in that time! Many Aussies in front of the box likely spat theirs after that start, to be sure. But they undoubtedly regathered composure when Australia II took the third race and came back to win the fifth and sixth after the Yanks won the fourth.

This forced a decider, the first time the great seafaring tussle had gone to seven races. Now all this was pretty much lost on us rug rats, but what wasn't beyond our capacity was that we were up at dawn, well before He-Man came on, and even before Dad whipped us up a round of hot Milos. Something big was happening—even Prime Minister Hawke was watching. Of course, a boat race in itself isn't all that thrilling, but the very idea that Little Old Us Down Under could take on the might of America—or at least the New York Yacht Club—and show them a thing or two despite their pedigree, well, that was worth the effort. I mean the New Yorkers had been polishing the cup with spittle for 132 straight years! It's a wonder that Australia—or any other country for that matter—even bothered to slip on the Sperry Topsiders and hoist the mainsail.

But they did, and all of us who saw it can smile with nostalgia. Reading about this event on the National Maritime Museum website recently, I couldn't help but see the funny side, picturing an irate American crew losing it at each other as Australia II took the lead. According to the account, there were some crucial moves by the Aussies and this was one of them:

As they closed on the last rounding mark at the bottom of the course, with both boats on opposing gybes the moment came when Australia II passed ahead of Liberty, still sailing faster and in phase with the small wind shifts. Choosing the right timing Australia II gybed down and then back again to the mark, rounding 21 seconds ahead of a horrified US team on Liberty.

Honestly, Dennis Conner looked like the kind of guy that could yell a pirate into submission. I think this left an impression on us tikes, because here, with televised sport, we could witness great drama and the possibility of our own potential. But perhaps more accurately and without the sentimentality of it all, the Conners, Kiwis and comebacks simply gave us good stories that were slightly more compelling than those with wolves, witches and gingerbread men.

We Could Be Heroes

The makeshift jungle in our backyard was the ideal place to lie and wait for the enemy to approach. Who were we fighting? Well, whoever came around to play on a given day. Friends, cousins, neighbours—each armed with water pistols, or Nerf guns, maybe even some water bombs. Whatever the troops could get their sticky little fingers on. Like most kids growing up, the backyard was where we imagined Platoon-level heroics.

So, missions carried on, gratefully in the safest place a kid can ever imagine—the space within the fences of his own home. It was perfect. The foliage was dense, the grass tall, the heat stifling.

Visibility was low on any given summer afternoon, sometimes because of the blur of hot air around us, other times due to the heavy rain that fell with a sudden thunderstorm. This was an exciting battleground for a ragtag battalion of suburban punks acting out their wildest fantasies as Commando or Rambo. Sure, we didn't have army boots, but Adidas and LA Gear high tops were sufficient. And Mum's lipstick stood in for the black camouflage typically painted on by Arnie and Sly. Hey, we felt tough and that's all that mattered, even if we did sport bright pink Catchit surf t-shirts and floral Okanui shorts. We'd muddy our clothes as we crawled stealthily through the weeds and leaves, holding our breath in anticipation of a water bomb sneak attack. "Oh, crap!" Splat! Splash!

Every generation has its heroes, be they real-life model citizens or the more common celebrity type that only plays the brave protagonist on screen. The eighties had a broad offering to be sure, including Nelson Mandela and Lady Di, as well as politicians like Ronald Regan and for some, Bob Hawke here in Australia. Some looked up to Warren Buffett, others simply adored Mr T. There was Yoko Ono, Bill Gates and Barbara Walters. Margaret Thatcher, Mikhail Gorbachev, Kylie Minogue, and Michael Jordan and yet, amid all those greats, it was a time of beefed-up mega heroes, too!

Hollywood had entered a new era at the turn of the seventies, where the shoot 'em ups and gangsters, fast cars, real-world horror and dystopian obsession were replaced by chiselled action heroes and their quest for good. They were large, muscular and proficient in monosyllabic dialogue. The decade kicked off with *Conan The Barbarian* slicing through the screen in 1980, then brought back *Rocky* for a third round in '83, had Michael Douglas swinging from jungle vines and unloading shotguns in *Romancing the Stone*, boasted Van Damme's martial arts artistry in *Bloodsport*, and saw a rogue Steven Segal slinking about in *Niko Above The Law*. It also showcased several Kurt Russell efforts that deserve their own book, really, not least of which was Kurt in an eye patch and with a weirdly gravelly voice in *Escape from New York*.

Stallone popped onto screens many times too, and it's tough to call out one above the other but certainly *Cobra* and *Over The Top* were notable offerings. And of course, there was our man Arnie, the most influential person out of Austria since Freud. Only Arnie wasn't necessarily a thinking man like the good doctor. Instead, his muscles gave rise to the theory that in eighties Hollywood all you needed were iron fists and a knack for cheesy throwaway lines to earn a star on Los Angeles' most famous pavement. Nobody mistook these guys for serious thespians, but that was fine with us. That they were rather cartoonish and sometimes hard to understand only endeared them further to my family. They had a vulnerability, we argued, and street smarts, lots of that. They also took care of themselves, worked out, ate well and kept their crew cuts trimmed. I feel like all this makes them ahead of their time.

Back in the eighties, these guys were a special breed, fantastical beasts roaming everyday worlds.

The funny thing about such huge heroes was that you wanted to act like them, recite their lines and come off as similarly indifferent when faced with any challenge. And yet, they always felt like such distant people, unreal and unattainable in every way. This is kind of what made having them as heroes okay because they weren't actually role models. We admired them but knew it was going to be a strange road to have travelled on if we ever found ourselves in a South American jungle on the run from a lost alien. And if we were ever seeking revenge against a bunch of street toughs with nothing but a few roundhouse kicks and a cynical view of the world, well we'd know that things might have come off the rails. Eighties action stars would indeed find themselves in places as far off as the Colombian or Brazilian jungles, but also in dusty Mexican villages, darkened New York back alleys or rough Chicago streets. They might get to Moscow or even Osaka. They could be hulled up in Cuba or shacked up in a Tijuana villa. And they'd almost always get caught up in a car chase across Los Angeles. Wherever there was trouble, big dudes with a heroic purpose were ready to whoop ass.

For us as skinny little kids, these people were larger than life. The over-pumped and wild-eyed heroes of the era were heavily armed and full of swagger. They typically had square jaws, dark sunglasses and some kind of cool jacket or trench coat. They had secret tucked-away weapons, chequered histories and revenge on the mind. These guys were loose, both with their firearms and dirty language, but generally didn't give away more than one grunt at a time. That meant romance was often an afterthought and the majority of the time on screen was about busting open lips. That's how we liked it! These guys were here to save the day, to make things right and quite often to rescue someone they cared about. Such fictional beefcakes were ideal hero material in our eyes. I'd even go as far as to stuff socks in my sleeves to help bulk up my biceps and might have even sprayed some of Mum's mousse in my hair to achieve a Schwarzeneger-level spike.

Neither Mum nor Dad had a trench coat, but a dark raincoat was a sufficient substitute.

You know that these megastars meant something to a generation when at the end of their eighties run they were allowed to open up a chain of restaurants: Planet Hollywood spun into our universe in 1991. They did very well in the early going and I think that was a testament to their cultural cache —this was a virtual universe of larger-than-life film stars who were most often depicted saving the world. It was a marketing dream come true! This type of hulking, shirt-off, tight-lipped and even sardonic eighties action character became the template for blockbuster movies from then on and this continues today.

I also want to point out that there weren't a lot of heroines in movies at the time, so their glaring omission here isn't intentional. There were many heroines we looked up to! As a matter of fact, I'd like to provide just a smidgen of balance to the equation by noting how much I followed and admired the original Wonder Woman played by Lynda Carter, whose portrayal of a very super lady was second to none in my mind. She kicked butt and took names and I couldn't wait for *Wonder Woman* reruns after school in the early eighties. I mean come on, she lifted cars and flew up incredibly tall ladders, outwitted punks and took down thugs. It was daring and dazzling stuff and deserved a special section in all Planet Hollywood restaurants. That the character was resurrected for the big screen in recent years is really tipping of the crown to the original woman of wonder.

The other type of hero that I haven't delved into here and that deserves a shout-out is the high school dweeb turned cool guy. If I'm honest, the dweeby guy or average Joe was more relatable to suburban kids and we were no different. Not saying I was a geek, folks, but I certainly gravitated towards the independent thinker who could turn on the charm, save the day and maybe win over the girl by the movie's end. Those sorts of films always made me feel like a little hope in real life could actually work.

Here I come back to Cusack, whose quintessential lovable loser was Lane Myer in the film *Better Off Dead…* Lane isn't doing so well and thinks himself better off dead when he's dumped by his girlfriend Beth before Christmas. But as he weighs up life, Lane realises he also wants to desperately win Beth back and hopes to do so by skiing the impossible K-12 Mountain. It's a great premise as you can see, but more importantly, Cusack's Myer eventually shows us that heroes can emerge from even the most humiliating or humble of circumstances. Of course, this was well-trodden ground and indeed an often-cited lesson for the kids of the time. Another of the most loved efforts at our house was *Summer School*, in which a group of underachieving high schoolers are forced to give up summer and redo classes with an equally lethargic and under-motivated physical education teacher, Mr Shoop. Hey, what can I say, hijinx ensues and the kids have a fun ride on their way to redemption with the help of their unorthodox tutor. It's light and breezy, and that's what was great about it. We saw the *everyday* hero in such simplistic plots and this mattered to the everyday kid.

Space, The Initial Frontier

If you grew up when I did, you'll know that space felt like a big deal. It wasn't just that the universe outside of our suburban homes seemed endlessly large or that many of the TV shows and movies shown inside our walls focused on space, including *Blade Runner, Aliens, Buck Rogers in the 25th Century*, *Doctor Who* and *Star Wars*, but that space had become a significant part of the lexicon. Politicians talked about it, writers and commentators covered it, and toy companies began to capitalise on it. One of those toys was our beloved Commodore 64, which I want to tell you a bit more about here. It might have just been a family-friendly computer heavily marketed at kids with 8-bit video games, but this thing was also a marvel of marketing genius.

Such was the popularity of the inexpensive and easy-to-use Commodore that the Guinness Book of Records has pegged it as the highest-selling computer of all time! That might have just been about timing—hitting the market when a ready and waiting crowd of junior computer nerds, aware of Atari and Nintendo Game and Watches, was primed for an action-packed personal computer experience. And yet, the boxy little machine was also armed with 65,000 bytes of RAM, which you might recall is the memory storage of a computer that it needs in the short term. So, the 'C64,' as it was called, was a big improvement on other computers, and this was reflected in its games which boasted multicolour sprites and cool sound effects.

Above all else, the science fiction category of its games fit in perfectly with Ronald Reagan's Star Wars defence system proposal and NASA's space shuttle era. Some of the C64's game titles included Space Firehawk, Space Rogue, Gradius, Galaxy, Space Harrier and of course, Space Invaders, among many others. With our joysticks in hand, poised for action, as our games loaded on tapes for many minutes on end, we imagined life in space, fighting intergalactic enemies, and the Commodore made it a near reality.

The big idea behind the C64 of course, was that it was a personal computer, meaning that its simplicity and relative coolness made it accessible to run-of-the-mill families such as our own. The computer, in the guise of this grey block with its black keys and recognisable rainbow logo, was no longer the domain of data scientists or your dorky uncle dabbling in computer chess. No, this was a new world, one in which the pyjama-clad seven-year-olds were taking over, battling 8-bitted Blasteroids and in Jet Pack Wars. Into the sprite-filled vortex we tumbled, gobbling on Toobs and downing our Fanta amid flashing lights and reams of code. Just as nobody cared about too much sugar at the time, nor did they worry about too much eye candy in the way of pixelated pulverisers and proton pills. The eighties truly ushered in home entertainment like nobody had seen it before and perhaps it went largely unnoticed that the protagonists of those entertaining adventures were children. Teens have always owned pop culture as long as it has existed, but it was this period of time that saw kids assume a central role in spearheading the popularity of gaming. Sure, Pac-Man and Frogger paved the way, but the eighties took the arcade into homes and the C64 was integral to this growing trend.

As much as timing played a role, I tend to think there was a kookiness to that 64 model that people loved. After all, it wasn't the only Commodore computer made—but it was the most famous. Why exactly? Probably because it was squarely aimed at the masses as the company's founder Jack Tramiel once said, whereas subsequent models targeted business people. This meant the price of it eventually dropped so low that it really became a staple of most households interested in gaming or basic computer programs. It may have looked a bit goofy, but in reality, this thing had all the bells and whistles needed for family gaming, including high resolution, multicolour, advanced sound effects as well as versatility in its software, providing for a cassette tape, floppy disk and cartridge-based content.

All of this combined saw the Commodore 64 sell for many years after its initial release in '82, which is kind of unheard of today given that every model of just about everything gets updated within years. I never thought it needed any improvement myself. After all, its limitations are precisely what led to its gaming innovation. California Games, anyone? Maniac Mansion? Last Ninja 2? Need I say more?

Items of Impact

Many things shaped our experience of childhood, not least of which was Mum making us wear short shorts and sandals for family photos, or Dad claiming that sitting too close to the TV would turn our eyes into little squares. If you'd seen us kids in those shorts you'd have planted your face square against the static-filled screen, too!

Other things were thankfully more attractive to the eye such as Eddie Van Halen's red, white and black guitar from 1984, which had an original basswood body, quarter-sawn maple neck, iconic hockey stick headstock and one pickup. This thing was a work of art with its 22 jumbo-sized frets along its fingerboard, and all those crazy stripes intersecting across the body like the icing on a delicacy from Donut King, which incidentally came on the scene in 1981. Known as Eddie's Striped Series 5150, it was considered a high-powered, top-performance guitar that only a true master could handle. Luckily, we never got our sticky icing-covered fingers on one, instead preferring the less complicated Air Guitar of 1988, with which we'd mime Robert Palmer's hit 'Simply Irresistible' for our parents after dinner. Soon enough, we'd graduate to a more advanced guitar, the aluminium Emrik tennis racquet strung around our shoulders with one of Dad's ties. This allowed for a lot more movement around the stage—the slightly raised floor beyond our living room. This was also the scene for other loosely-mimicked family favourites such as Billy Joel's 'Matter of Trust' and 'We Built This City' by Starship.

In between mini concerts, our house was always humming with one appliance or another. It was a time for hot household consumer items, where if you weren't watching something for entertainment, you were blitzing it in the kitchen to prepare a snack or were pressing a button to produce some other new-world comfort. There were little electronic gizmos like pocket radios, larger boxy tech such as personal computers and laser printers, incredible home studios because we now had camcorders, novelty telephones shaped like Garfield or a hamburger, brick-shaped cellular phones, sleek-looking answering machines, fax machines, pagers, electronic typewriters, personal copiers, food processors, bread makers, coffee makers, cappuccino machines, boom boxes, Swatch watches, an unending range of home exercise machines, oh, and pocket organisers, just in case you were struggling to stay on top of everything.

But amid all this, as well as our prized Nintendo and portable music players, there was one item that perhaps impacted our family above all else, at least for the duration of the eighties: our silver Panasonic NV-7000 VHS video recorder. All of my earliest film memories took place with this machine reproducing the images imprinted on the magical magnetic tape within our many recorded movies, from *Cannonball Run* to *Commando*, and *Return of the Jedi* to the return of Mahoney in *Police Academy II*. What really stood out about this Panasonic model, or at least the manual told us, was that it could record up to eight separate programs from the same or different channels. But that wasn't all, you could pre-plan these recordings up to 14 days ahead! That's right, no need to worry about missing our favourite shows anymore. This thing, if we had the smarts to work out how, could have recorded for us *The Smurfs* in the morning, *Gilligan's Island* in the afternoon and the Sunday Night Movie—usually along the lines of an edited version of *48 Hours* where we never heard Eddie Murphy actually swear, or perhaps a Stallone flick with any overtly violent parts cut out—without ever missing a beat. I'm telling you, gang, these were impressive times.

Sugar Rush

We've come a long way from the quick eats of a generation ago. Still, there was something superbly carefree about Sunday takeaway and snack-laden outings at the local fair back then.

While I'd never vouch for the same level of heavy dough, fried chicken and cheeseburger consumption with my own family today, I do miss the joy of it all—the frivolity of eating without over-analysis. Oh, and nobody would ever bother to take an iPhone snap of a pizza buffet for their blog, would they? Simple times perhaps!

I wanted to call out the little joys here—the indulgent sweet snacks of our childhood that made us so happy. Cornetto ice creams from the beachside kiosk, bright yellow passion fruit-iced vanilla slices from the bakery, white paper bags of red and green frogs from the milk bar and chocolate crackles at the school fete. Of course, most of these things still exist, but certainly, there are fewer supporters of such sweet indulgences now. I mean chocolate crackles are about as common as acid wash jeans, which is why I chose to highlight them in my title. Like most ten-year-olds in '87, I loved anything consisting almost entirely of sugar, and yet, my sweet tooth was also discerning enough to enjoy textured treats with colour and shape, many of which marked the most magical moments of our childhood. I'm thinking about post-Saturday sports gatherings at the park, birthday parties with your best pals, recess handball tournaments and family afternoons in a sun-filled garden.

Parties might just have been the peak of pig-outs because mums and dads back in the mid-eighties didn't regret mixing rice bubbles with melted marshmallows, or derive a sense of doom after scooping out orange quarters to replace them with jelly. They weren't perfect parents—nobody is, of course—of course, but they knew a thing or two about hosting kids' parties! My top-rated birthday event snack was the white crispy meringue, a puffed-up vanilla sugar decadence that offered a semi-soft surprise when you bit into the firm exterior. Sometimes these treats were covered with sprinkles or tiny series of candies inserted as a face, and other times they were just whipped up at their ends in a twirl. They were just a marvel of innovation, yes certainly centuries ago, but perfected by the 1980s parent with an eye for uncomplicated flavour.

Sugar has copped a bit of a hammering since. There's either too much of it or the wrong kind or maybe it's a fake sugar that's been inserted into the mix and that alone has caused consternation. Look, I'm not going to pick a side here—sugar-filled or sugar-free, but I will say there was less sweating the small stuff back in the eighties, at least when it came to the kids' party spread. It's a small miracle that Kit Kats and Crunchies have survived, really. As for the frogs, well I noticed the red ones are still leaping into the occasional welcoming mouth...but the green ones are a bit harder to come by. Maybe they just saw the writing on the wall and after the eighties, headed for the hills, hopefully somewhere where sugary things are still appreciated. Chocolate and candy brands are the sort of thing that most adults select in the jukebox of nostalgia above all else, and so deciding which era made the best is a fool's errand. But I think many will agree that the unabated run of junky food production in the eighties was a contributing factor to the mass consumption of candy shop favourites henceforth.

There are two converging storylines when it comes to the uptake of sweets sold at the time: one is the commercial promotion of foods to children made possible by the cutting of regulatory red tape. The other is the assortment of exciting new goodies created. The two things together made it a tasty time for kids. Then there's the nostalgia associated with the TV ads that initially introduced us to our favourite chokies and lollies. This brand association can't be denied. I still remember seeing Kit Kat ads with my family as we charged into the living room to catch the start of *Growing Pains*, where inevitably the kids in these types of programmes devoured similar treats. This was part of it and I suppose everyone was doing the same thing, or at least it seemed.

Well, Kit Kat was among the best when it came to spruiking its goods. You can search many of these promos online and see what was done in America or Europe, but I still love the Aussies ones most, especially those mid-eighties ones featuring an animated Kool Kat who sounds like a cross between cartoon greats Top Cat and Snagglepuss. In one scene, Kool Kat is unsurprisingly too hot in the Aussie sun and given that he might have hailed from New York as his accent indicates, he seeks the chill of a refrigerated Kit Kat chocolate. Simple and yet so excellently appealing to those with both a penchant for chocolate-coated wafers and anthropomorphic cartoon characters like me and my brother. Kit Kats back then also came wrapped in foil rather than plastic, which always made them seem colder out of the fridge. Not that they'd ever sit on that top shelf long enough to get overly cool.

Skittles were another standout because ad makers for the tiny candies were intent on making every commercial spot seem like a party. 'Taste the rainbow' cry the teenagers and cool adults in one series of ads, dancing around with their denim jackets and big hair, tossing Skittles in the air as if on an unstoppable sugar high. Indeed they were—we all were. It was a memorable time, a time in which a multi-coloured bag of chewy candy drops could be created and added to the pop culture landscape, as Skittles were in 1982. Skittles were also fun to share with your siblings or mates and I think a lot of candy purchases are made on this basis alone. Space Food Sticks fell into this category too because the fudge sticks were easy to break in half on the playground as you ran for your life in a game of bullrush. I do feel like eating on the run was easier in the eighties.

Eighty-two was a big year in lollies really, as Runts came along then and we never looked at fruit the same way again! The creators of these little fellas knew what they were doing from the get-go, inventing candies that are actually shaped like the fruits they purport to represent. Brilliant! Looking for a healthy dose of fruit pieces, Mum and Dad?

Look no further than Runts, intensely coloured and rock hard. But that just meant they lasted longer. In fact, in our home, Runts were hoisted up as one of the great uses of sugar in the era. Well done Willy Wonka's factory, we never doubted you, even when you yelled "Good day, sir!"

Now let's not forget Nerds here, folks. They popped up in '83 from Nestle, a wonderful time to devour little coloured sugar crystals in the movies, when *War Games, Superman 3, Trading Places* and *National Lampoon's Vacation* all arrived at the box office. These treats came in artificially flavoured cherry, watermelon, orange and grape—little nuggets of magic that were certainly suitable for jocks and nerds alike. They were and remain a staple of the popular primary school set because let's not beat around the pot of hot sugar syrup here—Nerds were a well-received oversupply of intensely engineered flavour in a convenient little box. Who but the greatest nerds of sweet science could conjure such a treat? Like Runts, these tiny gems were presented as lollies made especially for kids—as if there was any doubt—through the cool cartoon characters on the front of the packaging. This sort of thing really sums up the eighties advertising mind, a sort of dedication to silliness, overindulgence and complete neglect of diabetic issues. But listen, these experts weren't completely throwing caution to the wind. They separated the box into two compartments so that a seven-year-old could suitably ration their Nerd intake. Nestle was also smart enough to make Nerds cereal, often with plastic trinkets stashed inside, in case you were wondering. It was 1983, gang, and I'm not ashamed to say that it was a rip-roaring, candy-crunching time.

Lastly, it'd be negligent to forget the world famous Gummy Bears, everyone's favourite for a reason. They taste good, yes, but they also importantly appeared at the tail end of one of the eighties' best teen movies, *Ferris Bueller's Day Off*. The school bus scene that runs during the credits shows an unforgettable exchange between a young girl and Principal Ed Rooney when she offers him a 'warm and soft' Gummy Bear that's been in her pocket all day. The movie's main theme—Yello's 'Oh Yeah'—bops along in the background, when Rooney takes the red Gummy and tosses it away. It's especially funny because the gag is capped off by Rooney spotting some graffiti that says, "Rooney eats it!" Well played, John Hughes, surely a lover of fine candies, too.

Scary Stuff

The horror movie format of my formative years demanded either a weird mutant attack or the saga of a mad monster gone wild. On the one hand, citizens were on the run from crazed *Gremlins*, *Critters* and *Ghoulies*, while on the other side of town, there were neighbourhoods under siege from wolf men and slimy phantoms. Scary stuff could be found in all forms! Not to be outdone, there was a hybrid version too, a sort of a man meets ghastly idea, like Freddy Kruger in *A Nightmare on Elm Street* or Jack Torrance in *The Shining*.

Of course, the decade's extravaganza of horror highlights on the big screen went in many different ways and took on a multitude of shapes, from poltergeists and zombies to vampires and king-sized mutant alligators. All of the bases were covered, like a sticky and sprawling cobweb over an antique hallway lamp. It's worth recalling some of this popcorn-chewing fun because the horror, or at least Scary Stuff Industry, did very well in the era of excessive pop culture consumerism. People liked a bit of scariness and pants-wetting back then. They were primed for it. This isn't to say that previous eras of horror movies or toys for that matter, weren't just as creative or remarkable. But the eighties really seemed to be a climax in horror concepts and there was certainly a proliferation of scary films and accompanying paraphernalia. Michael Jackson's 'Thriller' video, for example, was a perfect piece of art for the time, a catchy blend of crazy and kitsch, and a wonderfully self-aware moment of popular music that transcended all other music videos at the time. Jacko's Thriller was a downright thrill, in both its beat and rhythm and also its horror-inspired choreography that included dancing zombies. It was really the first of its kind in music, where a pop artist took a chart song and turned it into a cinematic event.

Similarly, author Stephen King churned out some of his best horror titles in the eighties, propelling him to writing superstardom. This possibly never existed before King because his books seemed to sell on the basis of his word association—scary-cover-art-plus-scary-title can be a hit in the world of novels. But not all scary books have the name 'Stephen King' plastered across the front of the book. That's not to take anything away from the work—you could hardly have the success he had without writing blood-curdling yarns that pull you in like an enraged beast. But King's commercial appeal was perhaps apt for the times: an era that loved both the horror category and the selling of it. After some preliminary introductions to the genre in the seventies, this truly was a generation of people ready for even more bumps in the night.

For us kids, the toys were again the most important aspect of it all. I remember my horror-loving brother getting around with a creepy Freddy Kruger glove, which was pretty realistic for a piece of cloth and plastic. Then there were an endless array of rubber and latex masks he had, from mutated monsters to wolf men and of course ghostly zombie types. Halloween was a big event in our house and not in many others at the time. Back then only a few families seemed to even understand what the holiday was all about, which is why so many door openers turned us down on the offer of 'trick or treat.' We weren't fazed however, we just moved onto the next place, bags open and water pistols loaded with soapy liquid. There were other scary toys on offer, though they were usually more quirky than frightening.

Mad Balls were among my favourite of those, a very eighties idea to mould a disgusting face into a foam rubber ball so that it offered a dual purpose—to be thrown around the house and knock our parents' valuables off the shelf, but also scare the crap out of them when they pulled it out of a half-broken vase. My prized possession for a time was a Mad Ball named Screamin Meemie, an ugly grinning face sticking out its tongue impressed upon a rubber baseball. I just loved the idea that a baseball could look alive, though I don't think Mum agreed. I mean these things were advertised with the whole family in mind and even ran with the slogan, 'Freaky fun for everyone!' Well, almost everyone. Other balls cast a wider net, fishing for laughs with names like Freaky Fullback (a mutant football player), Bruise Brother (a biker with a battered helmet) and Wolf Breath, which is perhaps why our dog felt a kindred connection to this particular ball.

The makers of the Mad Ball series, AmToy out of the US, weren't satisfied with just oddly smelling foam balls—they wanted the whole enchilada. And soon enough, they went for a bigger helping of the scary toy market, adding comic books, video games and a TV show. Only in the eighties was such a broad approach feasible in a singular content category!

Such an elaborate strategy was not lost on other toy makers, who quickly came to see that a multi-pronged approach to marketing was the best way to maximise the interest in ideas like Care Bears, He-Man and Super Mario

Bros. He-Man is a particularly good case study, with the toy series preceding the cartoon TV show, which really wasn't the way things were done to that point. But once again the people behind the concept understood the market before it understood itself, and so they went about inventing both heroic (He-Man) and scary characters (Skeletor) in what would be a transformative toy that raked in $350 million for Mattel as of 1984, according to a *New York Times* report in that year. Throw in the towels, clocks, toothbrushes on top of the muscle-bound figurines and revenue was said to be closer to $1 billion, the same article noted.

I'm not using the 'transform' adjective by accident here folks, because Transformers soon followed and the likes of Optimus Prime and his good-guy robot crew would take on a nasty villain called Megatron who morphed into a gun of all things. Not sure that one would get out of the marketing meeting in 2024, but as I said, the eighties seemed to exist on a separate plane of the grandiose and gratuitous.

Of course, some parents from the time will disagree because the eighties saw an opening of the floodgates in toy advertising and other branded goodies for kids. It was in President Ronald Reagan's tenure that regulations were cut away like the packaging around a Kenner doll. This is a point worth raising (zombie reference intended!), for it was Reagan's new communications henchman that decided to let the industry self-regulate, essentially meaning advertisers could not just flog toys but also sell kids sugary cereal during their morning cartoons, and as they did with Masters Of The Universe, GI Joe and Transformers, create entire shows around toys to sell products. I honestly look back on the time with nostalgia, seeing a spilling over creativity in kid-centric concerns. So, you know, there are few complaints from my Converse-wearing, front-teeth-missing, bubble gum-chewing self, though I concede that mass commercialisation to children surely lightened the piggy banks of families everywhere, perhaps the scariest aspect of this whole tale for parents.

Hoop Dreams

While we took to the sporting grounds for soccer primarily, basketball quickly became a love affair in our home. It never superseded 'calcio,' but it was up there, like a soaring Michael Jordan throwing the ball down on the Cleveland Cavaliers in 1985. Ah, the Cavs, they were always such a solid outfit in the eighties, and yet against the swashbuckling Jordan, Cleveland's men were more like bumbling palace guards.

The NBA—now one of the world's most popular and lucrative sporting exports—seemed from a distant planet back then, an arena of combat that lived largely in our imagination because there was such little coverage in Australia at the time. But we did get a weekly contest courtesy of ABC sports via a green jacket-wearing, mop-topped TV presenter named Peter Gee. We'd never really heard of the bloke, at least not in the same way as other titans of the tube, like Ray Martin or *The New Price Is Right's* Ian Turpie, but we liked him. Gee was a bit stiff but he had some good lines from time to time and we really grew to appreciate his intros to weekly NBA accounts. One of his best followed a clip of a missed fast break dunk by none other than Air Jordan, to which Gee surmised, "Even Superman comes unstuck from time to time."

We were thankful for Pete and his perceptiveness though more than anything, we loved seeing the sport's biggest stars go around each week, even if in a truncated format that typically skipped past the slow parts of the game. There was

Jordan wagging his tongue and pulling on the hems of his shorts, of course, but also floppy-haired hick Larry Bird, the offensive maestro Magic Johnson, the loud-mouthed mega forward Charles Barkley and the aggressive yet agonised style of Patrick Ewing. There were so many others, but it was the sport itself that we really marvelled at—its scintillating pace, its array of attacking moves available to the best players and even the in-game commentary, somehow more crisp and creative than the voices of our local games, and at the same time able to amplify into hyperbolic cries over the vision of impossible dunks and dribbling moves.

We also collected NBA cards as a result, stacking up the 1989 Fleer series with a level of devotion only witnessed by those who saw us pore all over the '83 Scanlens rugby league stickers. The '89 basketball cards in this collection were made of very plain cardboard on which the player's vital stats—oddly including 'predicted' points and rebounds per 48 minutes instead of actual posted numbers—were accompanied by a short "Did you know?" section, regaling the player's best bullet point achievements. But when I think back on those cards, the reason we enjoyed them so much was because of the up-close photos, typically showing the player in a shooting pose or mid-dribble. These were hardly action-packed portraits like so many of the trading cards that followed, but rather more intimate stills which allowed us to see the player's facial expression, or maybe even how their moustache held up in the midst of a heavy third-quarter sweat. In a similar way, we adored the seven-foot posters of our favourite stars, chiefly Michael Jordan and Magic Johnson. These huge sheets of poster paper almost reached the ceiling of our room, with both Michael and Magic seemingly watching over us like archangels each evening. Okay, so their presence wasn't quite so mystical and yet we revered them and saw their prowess on the court as an evolved level of athleticism, surely only possible to the superhuman.

Then there was our indoor Nerf hoop drilled into the wall by Dad, on which we jammed Dominique Wilkins-esque windmill jams in our pyjamas and jiffy socks. Three-pointers were probably more our speed after a few collisions into the wall, and we landed more than a few after weeks and months of practice. The spongy Chicago Bulls-branded ball eventually had so much give in it that you could miss the hoop entirely, hit a dead spot in the wall and be quietly confident that it would slip down the face of the backboard and eventually through the net for three. Such plays were the stuff of genuine hoop dreams, folks! But of course, nothing was better than the real thing and Dad had constructed a makeshift hoop at the end of our carport, which it must be said was only about eight and a half feet high.

Still, we were well below NBA-level point guard heights and so this lowered basket—a netball hoop in fact—was ideally suited to our Larry Bird impressions and heated games of H-O-R-S-E. Oddly, that old mulberry tree protruded into the shooting space from the left side of the nearby garden bed, which meant any threes from the left needed to not only arc up from the low vantage point of our Muggsy Bogues-level stance but also through the forked branches of the tree. It was no mean feat, but eventually, we mastered it, sending our almost bowling alley smooth rubber Spalding ball into a desperate backspin en route to its final destination—the soft red, white and blue netting below our yellow hoop. The aluminium roofing of the carport would clang and clank as the ball careened into the cylinder, often sending the wooden backboard into a slight wobble and us to joyous high-fives.

All this was a far cry from the hoops we'd see at the Sydney State Sports Centre where the best team in the city, the Kings used to play. But it was good enough for us to mimic the moves of Mr Magic Steve Carfino, Sydney's silky skilled point guard, or Damien Three-o Keogh, the club's three-point marksman for many seasons. Those early days of the Kings were our up-close introduction to professional basketball and were filled with all the pomp of a Lakers game many miles away in Los Angeles, which is what I think they were going for. Even our point guard was called 'Magic!' The only thing missing were celebrities in the courtside seats and yet, we hardly cared about that, we were there for the dunks and dervishes, whirling through the western Sydney night against the enemy Tigers, Falcons and Spectres…oh my!

Backyard Bashers

Growing up in Australia has always included an introduction to cricket in the backyard, this wonderful though short-form of the game has been around for a long time. But like so many things, I'm willing to argue that in the middle of the eighties, a golden era of backyard cricket unfolded. How do I know? Well, I have no data if that's what you're after. But I do have anecdotal evidence which, on the one hand, relates to the passion for an Aussie team that included all-time greats such as Allan Border, Dean Jones and the Waugh brothers. On the other hand, I'd suggest the nineties ushered in changes to suburbia which saw backyards shrink, fences erected in subdivisions and spaces disappear altogether as McMansions upsized interior living. In other words, the eighties were a time in which backyard cricketers could excel on the sprawling pitches preserved for them. Times change but the records still stand!

Thankfully, unlike so many things I'm recalling here, backyard cricket continues to thrive across the country, albeit in more confined areas. Our beaches and parks have also offered enthusiasts lovely alternative venues, too, especially where unit blocks have replaced houses. But has the game changed? Not really. The whole thing has always been about quick glories. Setting up at the crease for a backyard cricket match was never about longevity or durability, but figuring out the fastest way to hit the most blistering shot.

For me in the summer holidays of '88, that shot was a short six-and-out, usually played towards the closest fence. Of course, some households didn't offer the short six that we were afforded in my family's yard. We had a relatively shallow six-and-out fence to the left, a deep six-and-out at the far end bordering the neighbour's driveway, and then a very difficult but glorious six-and-out boundary over our house. That was a shot really only worth trying if you were prepared to take the heat for potentially losing the tennis ball in the creek along the back of the property. Our friend John was always good for a fast ball, hard up the seam and dead on the chair that stood in for the stumps. He'd charge up the footpath that ran alongside the far end of our house, hop a couple of busted-up steps, and then complete the move on our paved play area by cocking the ball high and then rolling over the shoulder with Geoff Lawson-like prowess. The ball would rocket towards you, skim off the bricks and bounce up at your unprotected crotch, rendering you absolutely helpless—unless you managed to lift your bat an inch off the ground to try to nick it away for an aimless four behind. That was a safe play under the circumstances, and even more so when your grip on the bat was hindered by the sticky remnants of a melted pineapple Splice.

In fact, those Splices undid you in more than one way because if the heat set in, as it was prone to do on long January days, a second and third Splice might be all your little brain could focus on—the family jewels be damned. However, if you were savvy enough, and I like to think that in my floral board shorts and well-worn Reebok tennis shoes that I was, you'd simply close your eyes and thrust the bat out a second before John reached the crescendo of his bowl so that at least half of your bat might meet his maddening bullet of a bowl and ricochet it towards one of the six-and-out areas. The house was close enough and within view of the right-handed batsman, so that was often your best bet. If you could guide it up towards the roof that'd be ideal, but preferably the part, where the roofing changed angles so that it might bounce away from the waiting hands of a fielder ready for the one-handed grab off the roof, an easy out for a quick-witted ten-year-old. If you splayed it the wrong way you'd be forced to run and that was fine, but never all that easy when more than two or three of the neighbours were around. You'd be a sitting duck for a run out if the wicket was surrounded by nimble-footed sugar-boosted elves, each with arm enough to launch a shabby tennis ball at either end of an electric wicket.

Oh yes, electric wickets—the thorn in the side of every Aussie kid—being able to easily poke a ball towards the boundary but not speedy enough to escape the blitz of eager fielders. It was rare to find a batter with both speed and power. The speedsters usually knew exactly where to place it to defuse the electric run out, while the power strokers were so intent on belting it that they'd usually clear two fences, let alone a mere six-and-out.

It all ended with a pile of exhausted limbs flopping all over each other on the front step, another Splice or maybe a banana Paddle Pop in hand. The professionals wished they had tea breaks like this.

Road Trip-Ups

Hitting the highway with the family has been around since cars were big enough to fit the whole clan and a jumbo pack of Cheetos. So, somewhere in the early twentieth century, I suppose. But the endeavour has taken on different forms over the years since and perhaps none more pronounced than the advent of the station wagon, a car large enough to truly pack for a few days away, accommodating the family, their bags, bikes, surfboards and perhaps the dog.

Station wagons were on the scene well before most of us might know about them, but those long and wide wagons we grew up with didn't really hit the market until the sixties and seventies. Those cars brought in the big boot and eventually boasted the wood panelling within a steel frame. They were of their time and I believe peaked in the seventies, though carried on into the eighties. I say this because, after a few decades of road-tripping in larger family vehicles, the eighties represent a time, I believe, when loading up a large station wagon with everyone squashed in for a few hours had reached maturity.

It was maybe the last time the old-school road trip occurred in its simplest form, and by that I mean in a very boxy wagon with limited or no air conditioning, no cup holders, a radio or tape deck only, roll-down windows, less comfortable seats and in a colour like a pea green or mustard yellow that you wouldn't let your old aunt be seen dead in. If you weren't around for these road-bound holidays, let me assure you that you didn't miss out on much in the way of comfort. The old-school road trip, prior to the bigger and flashier SUVs of the late eighties, nineties and beyond, was an adventure unto its own. It was what I'd call a real road trip, where even if you weren't laying out in a tent or a cabin at the other end, you were still roughing it en route. There were also no digital devices to keep passengers entertained during the journey. Instead, your options were, a) ask your parents to play some music you actually liked, b) tackle a colouring or puzzle book, c) see how many jelly beans you could fit in your mouth, and d) simply stare out the window.

Okay, I lied, we did sometimes have a Nintendo Game & Watch we could fire up, say Donkey Kong, Parachute, or the incredibly addictive, Fire, in which you had to catch people jumping out of a burning building. There was no leaping from the family station wagon however, you were hemmed in for the long haul, basic entertainment on your person or not. Our Dad wasn't one to play louder music either, so we weren't hearing Springsteen or Aerosmith, nor were we likely to get Public Enemy, Tone Loc or Run DMC over the line. Maybe we could sneak a Billy Joel album by him on account of it having a lot of piano in the intros, but even then I don't think he cared for Billy's mood swings into a Ray Charles-like cry or even when he turned a little Paul McCartney on a song like 'You May Be Right.' No, we would have to compromise and that was okay, it was part of growing up then, accepting that you couldn't always have your own way. This is much harder to enforce in 2024! So, I do think today's kids would benefit from listening to a little Roy Orbison or Mario Lanza, or whoever fills those spaces now, just saying.

Ballads can be slow and jerk a few tears, but doesn't every road trip demand some self-reflection?

Finally, when you arrived at your destination, the red carpet wasn't rolled out I'm afraid, but more likely a patterned green carpet inside your motel room was, typically fraying at the edges. Yes, that's right—motels were the end game here, complete with a car spot directly outside your door. Not that you had Google to tell you this over your smartphone, of course. Rather, a faded, stained and typically torn around the edges copy of Gregory's street directory helped deliver your family to the motel's neon getaway. These humble little single or double-storey castles were bejewelled with an array of delights, too—usually a small TV of variable quality, a well-used bar fridge, a kettle and perhaps a fan in the summer. Around the concrete complex, you might have been able to toss a tennis ball or you could have jumped in the onsite swimming pool, should it have been issued with a splash of chlorine sometime in the past decade. But please know that I'm relaying all of this to you not as a file of complaints but rather as a series of fond memories.

The old-school road trip was fun because we had to make it so—the experience wasn't going to be handed to us on a silver platter. The only silver we might have seen was on the trimming of our eighties-era Volvo, which in my mind was pretty darn luxurious. I mean it had an ashtray for crying out loud, in which we could place the stubs of our chocolate cigarettes, Lucky Star brand. Though maybe my memory of that old blue wagon is coloured by the lunacy of being stowed away in the back seat (and boot) with my three siblings with no air con or personal entertainment to brag of for hours on end like it was no big thing. That's because it wasn't. Oh, we probably whinged and asked Dad *if we were there yet* a hundred times each hour. But we also knew that somewhere along the way he'd share a story of adventures he made while growing up.

And at about the halfway mark, he'd pull over somewhere quiet for us to have a ham sandwich and a sip of coffee from his thermos. Mum would tell us to read a book the rest of the way, perhaps a Roald Dahl classic like The BFG or The Witches, or maybe she'd humour us with a lengthy game of eye spy, and things didn't get much better than all of that.

Back to the Future

So much of life is looking forward that it's nice to look back. The family home I grew up in meant a lot to me, and clearly I don't want to let it go. I suspect this is the same for many people and perhaps not at all for others. But thinking back to that house, running around in my socks with my siblings, drinking Milo and imitating 'Uptown Girl' makes me happy for some reason. Besides the fun and laughs there's a sense of continuity in these thoughts. And that feeling deepens when I recollect some of the relics we unearthed in our home as kids. Take the old Super 8 camera we once found in Mum's closet—it was something our VHS-shaped minds couldn't compute. What was this thing? It looked like a laser gun from *Star Wars*, the sort wielded by one of those grumpy-looking bounty hunters. It was a portal to the past, a grainy-looking glass reflection of our world, just a short time before we were born. I loved the connection to both the silent images Mum and Dad had made and to the artefact itself, which is why we scurried up to the local chemist soon after finding it to buy some new Kodak film. The bloke behind the counter must have thought we were mad. I think we also got some jelly beans just so he didn't think we were weirdos.

Soon afterward, we were making our own movies, pulling on rubber masks and acting out scary chases through the park. We filmed basketball trick shots, daring skateboard moves down the driveway and ninja fights in fleecy black tracksuit pants. Tony Scott would have been proud. But this wasn't about movie magic, I don't think, but rather some attempt to add our experience to that of our parents.

A similar connection came about when we discovered Dad's seventies-era video game console that offered very rudimentary versions of tennis, squash and soccer. It wasn't an Atari machine but some other rip-off with these 2D games built-in, an unstylish computer system for a brown and beige decade, I guess. And yet we could miraculously control the little white lines that hit the square-shaped ball bouncing around the screen. So, before the C64 or Nintendo, this seemed like black magic! The screen was indeed black, though the magic really only lasted a few turns.

Finally, like King Arthur yanking Excalibur out of stone, we pulled Mum's old wooden Wilson racquet from the back of a cupboard and tennis revealed itself to us in a flash. What a brilliant piece of craftsmanship, its red and white painted finish catching our eye like a blade shimmering in the sunlight. Quickly, our curiosity led us to the likes of Borg and McEnroe, and the artistry such a tool might manufacture in the right hands. But if we were to truly imitate Johnny Mac, the most appealing of tennis stars to our young eyes, there was simply no way we could smash Mum's delicate wooden beauty into the ground. That's when Dad's workmanlike aluminium Emrik racquet won us over. While it was far from glamorous, it was well-suited to out-of-reach volleys and line-call tantrums.

I really like to think about the passing down of such everyday things. Even if just shared briefly, the experiences stay with us. Like a Schwarzenegger flick on the big screen or a memorable Pepsi ad on the small one, or even a plastic toy with barely a moving part, good ideas stay with us. And that's pleasing to dwell on and daydream about. I'd say that's why Doc ultimately invents the time machine in *Back to the Future*—to connect up all those points in time that shape us, but perhaps unexpectedly, also carry us forward.

Afterword: The Gen X Fantasy

Writer Douglas Copeland said in 1987 that Gen X didn't want to concern themselves with social pressures, money or status, which sounds about right. But it's also a little confusing because our youth came at a time when new kinds of social currency were emerging, including an obsession with making money! In my mind, the kids of Gen X, let's say those born in the mid-seventies or early eighties, possibly didn't care much about money or status in the way the adults of the eighties did—the Gordon Gekkos and Jordan Belforts of the world, if you will. And yet we *did* seek something—a taste of modern commercial cache, perhaps. I say commercial here because I think that's the difference between sixties leather jacket defiance and slick-haired bravado, or the self-expression and search for alternative meaning in the seventies. The pendulum swung away in the eighties towards a capitalist vibe, where mass consumerism took hold of dual-income families. This does suggest a drift towards money and status—for some, at least, but also gave rise to new types of cultural opportunities. So, you can see why as a Gen Xer, I'm perhaps more concerned with the fun ideas that a wealthier society provided than that of eighties-style power-grabbing.

We kids at the time just wanted to enjoy the incredibly interesting world set up around us. It was a universe of exciting new technologies as I've described, of fictional stories that revealed the infinite possibilities of faraway galaxies and metaphysics, but also the immediate safety and comfort of homes filled with 'mod-cons' like the slick kitchen appliances, televisions, VCRs and bulky stereo systems. If you were lucky enough to live in a middle-class home or better, then yes, the money and status were built in. However, this isn't about a relatively high standard of living per se, but a rather imaginative pop culture coexisting with a very busy economy.

How can we compute those competing interests, exactly? Maybe we can't, but we can say that while young Gen Xers grew up in a time that had its fair share of issues, they were lucky to be the beneficiaries of a very modern age, one in which they could mostly be preoccupied with the varied cultural cues around them. This all makes sense if you think about it: we knew how the war and post-war generations felt. They lived through hard times. And I'm not sure they experienced the same siloed comfort or naivety as us given they always had an eye on what global horror lurked around the corner. By contrast, eighties kids living in good communities surely never felt that. You might say there was a fair bit of optimism in suburbia, even during Cold War stand-offs and plummeting share prices.

For this, I'm grateful, especially given the crapshoot the world has found itself in since 2019. Maybe we look back at the state of things in the mid-eighties and appreciate what was going on with all our light-hearted distractions. For example, when Steven Spielberg and George Lucas came up with Indiana Jones, they must have known kids around the world would be willing participants in such old-fashioned adventure, but also that they would actually embrace the fantasy and play at home as Indiana Jones, too. That was the difference between an eighties-made character like Indy and the more classical Dick Tracy or Buck Rogers. Yes, all wore hats and had catchy one-liners, but Indiana came at a time when fantasy was more closely aligned to reality, due both to better filmmaking technologies, but also the merchandising strategies at hand. Together, this gave fans a tangible connection to the characters like never before. Toys were central to this connection. As they did with their Star Wars toy lines, Kenner brought out an Indiana Jones range, complete with bullwhip, satchel and gun holster. There was also a Marion figurine that came with the funny little monkey from the first film. Things didn't end there. Kenner also offered a map room play set, a well of souls set and streets of Cairo scene. I mean if that didn't immerse you into the fantasy nothing would. What I'm saying is the creators went to great lengths on this front. Guess what? Distraction was a popular tactic. Just to be on the safe side, the filmmakers also employed the gang at Nintendo to take Indy into a pixelated format. Indiana Jones and the Temple of Doom by Nintendo hit the game shelves in 1988 and while it wasn't a smash hit, it still put player-one in the box seat—or beanbag—if they sought to become Indy, even as a mere sprite. And so, amid all this activity, Gen X's conundrum was whether it could remain money and status agnostic, while also devouring the fantastic temptations before us. I think we did okay. We were coming up in a world where maybe some did think greed was good. But the other side of the coin was that there was competition in everything, between the movie makers, sneaker designers, toy creators, candy brands, soft drink producers and perhaps most noticeably between video game manufacturers. In fact, the race between Nintendo and Sega to win kids' hearts was unlike anything that came before it and, in a funny way, epitomises the whole era. I mean, in which other time would a pair of ludicrously athletic Italian plumbers and a super-speedy blue hedgehog have fought for global cultural supremacy? It's hard to imagine society accepting this outside of the whimsical 1980s.

Frequently Asked Questions

What was the greatest year of your childhood?

Wow, that's a tough one. I'm going to go with '85: The Breakfast Club, Huey Lewis and The News, Dire Straits, Madonna and Wham, Nintendo, WrestleMania, Growing Pains, Madballs, Pound Puppies and of course, the souped-up DeLorean in the greatest action-comedy of all time, *Back to the Future*. Can you think of a better run than that? Well, maybe '87 because I was old enough to really embrace long summers on my skateboard. I remember the music that year, which included 'Livin' On A Prayer' and 'Walk Like An Egyptian,' as well as movies that meant a lot to me like Spaceballs and *Planes, Trains and Automobiles*. Plus, legendary TV shows like The Teenage Mutant Ninja Turtles and The Simpsons started that year. Not bad, eh?

Which 80's artefact that's come back in the 2020s makes you the happiest?

There are so many really, but it's hard to look past those superb white Reebok tennis shoes. I see them everywhere now and I can't believe they're popular again. When I was eleven, I loved them, but I also weighed the same as a bag of potatoes and so never noticed how uncomfortable they could be after a lengthy walk. Are Gen Zers not spending as much time on their feet or something?

What are the best slang words from back in the day?

I've got three short ones for you: Rad. Ace. Tops. Enough said.

Who were the funniest characters from those movies you mentioned?

Are we talking real or animated? I mean this is a loaded question because I could give you some genuine real-life clowns. Okay, let's go with Fletch (Chevy Chase). Del Griffith (John Candy). John Winger (Bill Murray). Animated? Garfield or both Calvin and Hobbes.

What's the most iconic item of the eighties?

It has to be the Walkman. Few things were as revolutionary and most weren't as cool. Certainly, the Nintendo mattered to us kids of the eighties so that's right up there as well. How can you choose? I mean there are pizzas hot pockets for the microwave too, but I'll give Sony the gong.

Who was your favourite athlete growing up?

That's an impossible question. I probably have 27 favourites and some who I reflect on from time to time simply because of one play they made. So, that would bring my tally to about 53.

Okay, okay… I'll go with John McEnroe simply because he is emblematic of the times and if there is such a thing as sporting genius, he's it.

Which fashion item from your youth has proven most timeless?

I talked about big and baggy shirts. They have endured—somehow! And there are the sneakers, which have come back without any change, which is sort of strange. But ultimately I'd say the denim jacket. Who knew? It's sort of a ridiculous idea in a vacuum. And yet there it is, your pants are suddenly on your torso. Maybe, it's ingenious after all.

Which brands are the most eighties for you?

Well, you know how I feel about Pepsi. Nintendo again, but of course, there are many others that while not originally of the eighties per se, were hyped and heightened in that decade. I mean the Volvo station wagon was very eighties. So were techy things made by the likes of NEC and TEAC. How about Adidas sneakers? They were and are sooooo eighties. Lacoste is another one that for some reason was very *then* but also seems so very now. Maybe it never left. I also reminisce about Lotto soccer gear, Kenner toys and Hanna Barbera cartoons. M&Ms, Polly Waffles, jawbreakers, Wizz Fizz, Mellow Yellow and Rainbow Paddle Pops. Again, most of these things came before the decade, but in the eighties childhood, they were front and centre.

Were there any other cars from the period worth mentioning?

My other favourite is the 1979 Porsche 928, especially the one Tom Cruise drove in *Risky Business*. That car just looked ultra-cool, as I've mentioned. I know I'm not the only one that thinks this either because some cashed-up movie geek forked out AU$ 2.6 m for the thing at auction in 2021. Seems like a bargain to me! One more car I'd like to call out here is the sleek and sexy 1974, Lamborghini Countach LP400, perhaps even more sublime than the model I recalled earlier from *Cannonball Run*. What's most remarkable about this vehicle is that it appeared as a blue-lit hologram in the short-lived TV show, *Automan*. As a seven-year-old, I loved this program, mostly because Automan's car—you guessed it, Auto Car—was such an insanely flashy and fluorescent crime-fighting blur on four wheels.

Which politician epitomises the era?

The obvious answer here is Reagan. His confidence in America and its exceptionalism after the seventies was *so* eighties. He was right for the times in a sense, known to be pretty tough, optimistic and maybe above all else, a courageous character. I mean you'd have to be if you were shot and simply brushed that off to get on with your job. I know this is a very narrow answer, but I was a kid and I can only really recall bits of the world's story here folks. The history books do highlight the important role Mikhail Gorbachev played in ending the Cold War, so of course, Gorby gets a shout-out, too. Well played, mate.

Which major sporting event sticks out from your childhood?

In my home that would have to be the '86 rugby league Grand Final between my Parramatta Eels and my brother's Canterbury Bulldogs. It was a grudge match and a battle of attrition that produced a sleep-inducing 4-2 score. But we were wide awake and glued to the telly because a hard-nosed grind-it-out footy game was a thing of beauty in our house! My brother undoubtedly regretted that the Dogs only produced two points, but I'm certain he enjoyed the ongoing rivalry as much as I did, win or lose, and that this game was filled with some of the all-time greats such as Steve Mortimer and Peter Sterling.

Away from local footy, there were so many magical sporting events, from the aforementioned '84 Games in LA to the '86 soccer World Cup in Mexico. There was Magic Johnson's Lakers tussling with Larry Bird's Celtics throughout the decade, as well the many Super Bowl appearances of the San Francisco 49ers. And we can't leave out the 1980 Wimbledon final in which Bjorn Borg defeated my guy McEnroe. Too many events, too many moments to rank, the eighties offered a sporting champagne supernova and that's all before considering a bloke by the name of Michael Jordan.

What were the stereotypes before people cancelled them?

I mean where to start, there were many, including jocks, yuppies, fitness fanatics, geeks, preppies, motorheads, fleabags, potheads, guidos, brains, weirdos, rockers, mods, dweebs and suits. These sorts of classifications are indicative of eighties cliques or the labels ascribed to certain teenage types at least. As semiotics expert Marcel Danesi says in his writing, belonging to such a clique entailed acquiring the necessary characteristics by osmosis. He notes that a teeny-bopper who sees themselves as a hard rocker will eventually develop a 'hard' personality. This was a thing gang, you can't believe it, can you? But it makes sense. The semi-confused teen in Danesi's example would start with an attitude, maybe pick up a few choice words, slip on some ripped jeans and even grow his hair. You know the type—maybe it's you. Hey, we've all been there, but what I'm saying is the eighties really ran with this sort of stuff and we know that it resonated in artistic and cultural circles as a result. The great John Hughes was maybe the best at representing these types of different young people in his work, the most renowned being the movie, *The Breakfast Club*.

What were the best posters on your walls as kids?

It was wall-to-wall glossy ephemera, so where to begin? You can hardly go past the six-foot-six Michael Jordan poster, complete with a tape measure so you could match yourself up against Mike. There were also movie posters and I seem to remember both *The Lost Boys* and *Die Hard* taking pride of place. But to be honest, there were so many great posters from back in the day, ones that we wished we had, but never seemed to be available in the Tri-Star Video spare poster bin. We'd rush to the bin so excited at the prospect of a fresh, crisp, shiny poster to take home, only to be brutally disappointed when all that was on offer was a no-name B-grader like John

Travolta's eighties non-eighties hit, *The Experts*, or maybe George Lucas's famously wild miscue *Howard The Duck*. Where was *Nico Above the Law*? Or how about *Lethal Weapon*? *16 Candles*, perhaps? No chance of those at Tr-Star, poster hounds were better off up the road at the larger and well-stocked Video Ezy. Listen, we stood by Tony at Tri-Star. He put his best posters on the wall of his shop—that's really thinking about the customer experience.

You talk a lot about pizza and burgers, but what other takeaway meals were top of the list?

I can't overlook our favourite Chinese restaurant growing up, Mandarin Kitchen. It was a small takeaway joint with super-fast service and a friendly lady at the front desk scribbling orders down like she was working a Wall Street stock market floor. Well, we took advantage of both Mandarin's skilled front desk and its cooks, ordering beef with black bean sauce, sweet and sour pork and honey chicken without exception. Dad always ensured we also got multiple boxes of stir-fried rice as well as prawn crackers. No order was complete without prawn crackers, those bright pink chip-like goodies with an indiscriminate flavour, not quite prawn, but not unlike prawn. We miss you Mandarin.

What else stood out about eighties advertising?

The best ads from back then catered to people who liked bunkering down with a few comforts—those who sought some headspace to put up their feet with a Diet Coke and pop on a movie in the old VCR. Meanwhile, the kids were invited to block out the world with their Sony Walkman, White Snake or REM blaring through those bright fabric-coloured headphones. Many of the ads we grew up with offered a sort of refuge. They were 'at-last' solutions, with the smallest and most trivial product typically given a sense of over-importance like never before. The ads had far too many knowing glances amid warm lighting. Comforting arms around shoulders set to stirring music. Buoyant mops of hair on hunky dudes and blow-dried Charlie's Angels look-alikes. That was the eighties 'sell.' The personas were polished and stylised, sure, but they didn't need your approval. That's what I liked about them.

Why do you think people are leaping back into the retro vortex now?

Well, writing about the eighties is an entertaining exercise. A lot happened. Eighties culture author Chris Clews calls the decade a high point of creativity because it was quite possibly the last time ideas could reach the consumer before the marketing henchmen took full control and tested the absolute crap out of them. In other words, the eighties were a bit rough around the edges, things weren't perfect, and they were loose. And the money people greenlit a lot of wild ideas. Maybe it was because there was plenty of cash to go around, or maybe it was because mass production almost guaranteed mass consumption, but brands didn't worry so much about a lack of return. The public was willing to fork out their hard-earned moolah for just about anything half-baked, as long it delivered some playfulness, a touch of the fantastic or indeed a future so bright that you had to wear shades! 80's shades to be specific, the type that were a little large and had reflective lenses or those silly plastic ones with slits in between and no actual lenses. That's the sort of ridiculous idea I'm talking about.